Introduction

We really needed tax reform. I have been advocating for it for years.

What was proposed instead was HR-1 (which is now known as PL 115-97), which was labeled as the *Tax Cuts and Jobs Act.* The problem is that this law is going to hurt the US economy. Oh, I know we were promised that the economy would grow and make us all richer. But, just in the second quarter of 2018 alone, government collections are down more than $ 100 billion (a reduction of about 1/3 from the same quarter last year)- even with the economy still growing.

But, that doesn't change the fact that the tax code has been changed. And, we need to know what the code provides- to ensure that we can pay the lowest amount of taxes required by law. So, the above paragraph will be the last mention of what's happening with our economy.

Because of the way the law has changed our tax structure, the first part of this book will discuss the taxation of businesses. After all, most businesses in the US involve what is called pass-through entities- unincorporated businesses (Schedule C filers), partnerships (Form 1065), limited liability corporations (which may file Form 1065, 1120S- but some operate as non-pass-through entities and file Form 1120), and S corporations (Form 1120S).

If the bulk of the businesses operate as pass-through, we need to understand how the taxes for such businesses work- and then deal with the "pass-through" fund afterwards. In other words, unless we are a W-2 employee, a retired individual, or a professional stock investor, our businesses set up how we file our personal taxes.

But, if you ARE a W-2 employee (that means you get a W-2 from your employer) or are retired (income is recorded from stocks, bonds, and Form 1099 for dividends, interest, and pensions), you might just want to jump to Section 2, Chapter 7. The first sections of this book won't affect you at all.

Section One: Business Taxation Issues

Chapter 1: Business Entity Choices

PL115-97, the Tax Cuts and Jobs Act, has changed the way we think about business entities. Because, dependent upon our income levels, some of our pass-through income will never be taxed. As our personal adjusted gross income changes- and dependent upon the kind of business services or products we sell, that benefit evanesces. So, we need to consider what sort of business charter we should use – at least for the next 8 years or so.

For years, most financial advisors recommended that their clients set up LLC's (this stands for Limited Liability Corporations. If there is only one owner in the LLC, the Internal Revenue Service (IRS) considers this business to be disregarded. No, that doesn't mean the IRS doesn't care about it or how much revenue it makes; it just means for tax purposes, this entity can't stand alone- the income and expenses are reported to the IRS using Schedule C, attached to a 1040 (the personal income tax reporting form). Yes, the LLC provides the owner protection against personal wealth and debts and liabilities are not chargeable to the owner. (Please note that if you personally guarantee a loan for the business or pledge any personal property as collateral, you've pierced the corporate veil yourself. That pledge makes you personally liable. But, a lawsuit from a customer or another entity can only attach the assets of the LLC itself). Of course, if you don't operate your business professionally- like not filing annual reports or co-mingling business funds with personal funds (there must be separate business and personal accounts)- then the veil is easily pierced.

An LLC with two or more members can be classified for tax purposes as a partnership (we'll explain one big difference later on), an S-entity (pass-through business), or a C-entity (a corporation taxed separately, with no pass-through provisions to the owners, other than dividends, which are paid AFTER the corporation pays its taxes).

Businesses with two or more owners can also register with their local government and form a partnership. These entities stipulate who owns what- in other words, the partners own specific portions of the firm. The partners can be equal (if 2, that means 50-50) or the partners can own from a small portion to 99.99% of the business. An LLC that operates as a partnership is different- the members of the LLC can stipulate different percentages of profits and capital (each and every year) as splits among themselves.

Schedule C Entities- Unincorporated businesses or Disregarded LLC

The Schedule C is filed along with one's personal income taxes, Form 1040

Folks who start a side business (admittedly, some of which grow into full-time pursuits) normally operate as sole proprietorships. These businesses report their income and expenses on Schedule C of their 1040 (as shown above).

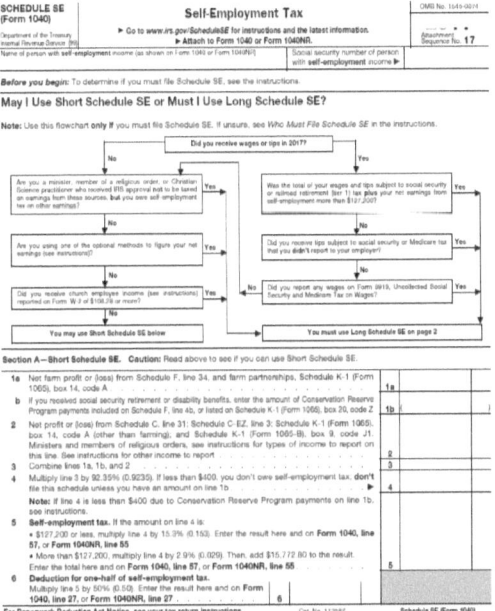

The business owners are obligated to pay employment taxes (Social Security and Medicare) on their net profits (at the rate of 15.3%), which would be reported on Schedule SE. A copy of the Long-Form Schedule SE is found above this paragraph.

As a result of the new tax law, through Calendar year 2026, 20% of the business' net profits will NOT be subjected to income taxes. Actually, that's not quite accurate. Only if the owner of this business has an adjusted gross income of less than $ 315K (or $157,500 if the owner is single), will that apply. As one income increases, that benefit simply gets erased.

Limited Liability Corporations (LLC's) and Partnerships (more than one owner)

More sophisticated businesses or individuals or folks who have partners would form an LLC (limited liability corporations) or a partnership. (By the way, if two or more individuals operate a side-business together, then that would be a partnership, not a Schedule C filer.)

[Form 1065 U.S. Return of Partnership Income]

Such businesses folks report their income and expenses on Form 1065. This is a business tax form, completely separate and apart from the personal income tax form, Form 1040 and its schedules and forms.

LLC's that have not notified the IRS they plan to operate as S or C entities may pay salaries or wages only to employees they hire. The partners who own the partnership or the LLC are not allowed to receive a salary. The owners of such entities receive their profits (the net income after expenses) as "flow-throughs"; the net profit is taxable to them as individuals (via the business K-1 of Form 1065).

S-entities; LLC's or corporations that have chosen the S designation

A Partnership K-1 form

The income reported on the K-1 is then incorporated onto Schedule E, page 2 of the 1040 personal tax return). And, the profit (as shown in box 14) is also subject to employment taxes (15.3%) on Form SE (shown above). Like the sole proprietorships, these folks also have that 20% pass-through tax holiday, if their income is below the limits ($157,500 for single taxpayers, $ 315K for marrieds; if one files separately from one's spouse [the designation is called married filing separately or MFS], the limitations on the pass-through exemption cut in at adjusted gross incomes of $157,500 each).

S-Corporation form

As I've alluded to a few times, some LLC's have filed various forms notifying the IRS that they wish to operate as corporations and be taxed as S or C entities. Other firms incorporate and notify the IRS they wish to operate as S entities. S used to stand for "small", but many large firms operate under the S configuration. These firms pay all staff- as well as their owners- salaries. (*Please note those shareholders must be earning "reasonable compensation" – income that reflects the training and duties of the owner- or the pass-through income may be fully taxed as "compensation" and not dividends. The determination of "reasonable compensation" is not one that fits the mission of this book. But, you are welcome to seek out the term in the author's blog, (https://www.adjuvancy.com/wordpress/reasonable/), among other places, if you are interested to learn more.)

The revenue and expenses of the business are reported on Form 1120S (shown above) and the net profits are apportioned among the stockholders (reported on the business K-1, shown below) and are taxed as part of Schedule E for the taxpayer. Like the LLC's above, these folks get 20% of their profits tax-free, if their income is under the limits stipulated above.

K-1 form for an S entity business

C Corporations (conventional corporate entities)

Finally, many firms develop C (or regular) corporations. These businesses do not pass through any income or tax-free dividends to the stockholders. Instead, the businesses are taxed as separate entities and any transfer of cash or benefits to the stockholders arrives in the form of taxable dividends. As of 2018, the tax rates for corporations have changed. Net profits will be taxed at 21% (*no more 15% tax rate for those with smaller (almost non-existent) profits*).

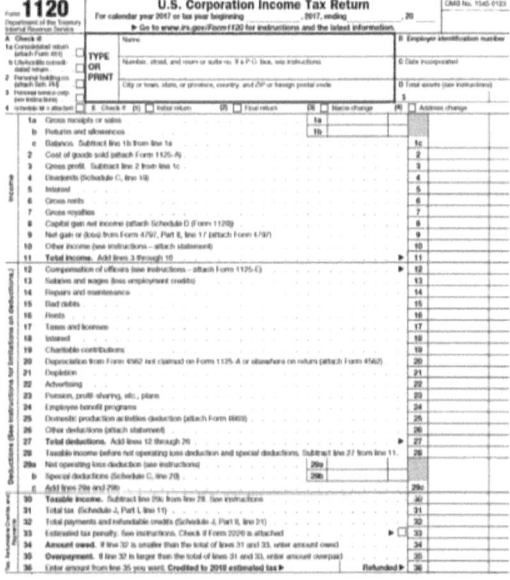

Form 1120, for Corporate Entity Filing

So, you can see that many of the upper middle-class business owners may want to consider a conversion to a C entity. After all, the pass-through firms need to pay the owners a reasonable salary- and, it's not clear (unless and until the IRS develops regulations) that C corporations must afford their owners reasonable compensation- unless they are professional service corporations, where the regulations do apply. Because the tax rate on corporate income is now 21%- our thought processes must change. Because if we have $ 500K of pass-through income (after salaries are paid)- and we are in the maximum tax bracket for individuals, there is a considerable savings. The tax on the $ 500K for a C corporation will be at most $ 105K. And, if we are in the $ 390,000 or more personal bracket, the personal taxes on that 20% pass-through (which has been eliminated) could be around $ 150K. We can place the $ 50 K we save in taxes into a profit-sharing plan for withdrawal when we retire. (There are many other tax strategies; this is but one.

What does this all really mean?

Now, that we got those preliminaries out of the way, let's consider why there may be new questions we must answer to choose among entities. We'll consider four separate scenarios. (*Even though I'll be using examples using unmarried taxpayers, you can basically double the numbers for married couples filing together and get the same results. And, as long as I'm saying this- even if you NEVER considered it before, you now MUST consider the Married, Filing Separately [MFS] status, because this 20% pass-through credit has income limitations- and filing separately may be the way to not lose the benefit for some higher-income couples.*)

Scenario 1: *Business nets $ 25000 (not including any salary or self-employment taxes)*

Scenario 2: *Business nets $ 75000 (not including any salary or self-employment taxes)*
Scenario 3: *Business nets $ 157,499 (to keep the $ 157,500 threshold on the other side and not including any salary or self-employment taxes)*
Scenario 4: *Business nets $ 314,999 (not including any salary or self-employment taxes)*
Scenario 5: *Professional Business nets $ 314,999 (not including any salary or self-employment taxes)*

Five Scenarios detailed above

What we see from the above chart is that S entities generally provide the best net compensation schemes for the taxpayer. However, our scenarios have not included state taxes, because each state has different tax rates. More importantly, there are jurisdictions like

Washington, DC, New Hampshire, and Tennessee that tax S entities on their net income (*and then tax the individuals for the pass-through income; in essence the businesses are taxed as if they are C corporations, with pass-through dividends to the shareholders*). Which clearly would affect our decisions as to the type of entity (and, if we can, where we wish to form our business that) we wish to employ for our businesses.

Moreover, as the income from the business increases, the difference between partnerships, proprietorships, and S entities tends to disappear- at least as it applies to net revenue passing through to the taxpayer/shareholder.

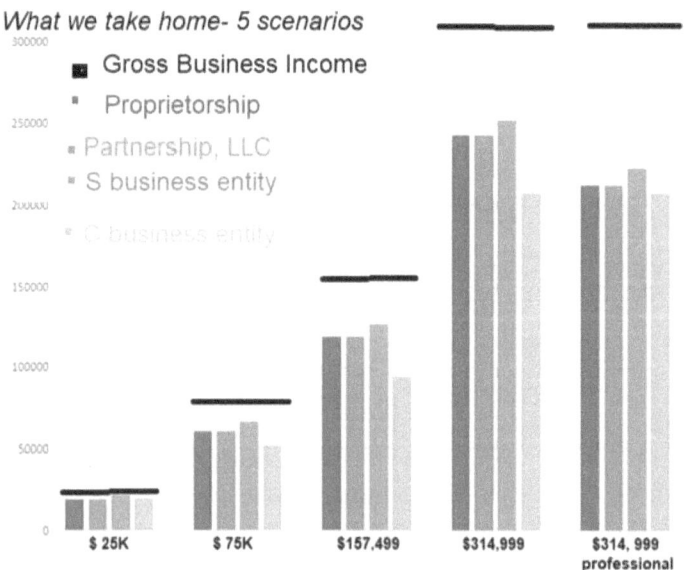

There are ways to reduce the taxes for business that have more than $ 100,000 of pass-through income. However, these are case specific. You should speak to you tax professional to see how they apply to you. Or, you could become one of our clients.

No matter what choice you make- remember that changing one's business type must be effected no later than 15 March to have the IRS approve that change for the entire calendar year. If you make the election later than that, the business entity must file two tax returns- one for before the change and one after- both "short-year" tax returns

Business Tax Rates

Prior to the change in tax law, corporations- just like individual tax payers- paid different marginal tax rates. The tax rates for CY 2017 are as follows.

Net Income	Marginal Tax Rate
< $ 50,000	15%
$ 50,001 to $ 75,000	25%
$75,001 to $10,000,000	34%
> $10,000,000	35%

2017 Tax Rates for Business

Moreover, if a company had more than $ 10 million in profits, there was no 25% nor even a 34% marginal rate. In other words, the entity was obligated to pay 15% on the first $ 50K and then 35% on the rest of its profits.

The tax changes provided a bit of good news for personal service corporations (PSC). These PSCs are firms that provide health services, legal representation, engineering, architecture, accounting, actuary services, performing arts, or consulting. These corporations had always been taxed at a straight 35%. (*This was the driving force for many of these firms forming LLC entities and NOT corporations!*) But, the new tax law depicts is no specification of a special rate for personal service corporations. They pay the same marginal tax rates as every other firm. (*That is not quite true- those PSCs that are pass-through (LLC's, partnerships, and S corporation), have special tax rules, as will be explained later on*).

The big change PL115-97 has wrought? The corporate tax rate has been permanently changed to 21% across the board. Yes, that means smaller firms are going to be zapped for 6% more taxes. And, those personal service corporations? They save some money, but still have a special flat rate of 25%.

Then, there's pass-through companies. Officially, pass-through companies are awarded a 25% income tax rate. And, since they don't pay any taxes, it means the stakeholders (shareholders or partners) in those companies get to pay those tax rates. BUT... It turns out that only passive owners of those firms will be eligible for that 25% rate. Oops- there are even more exceptions. Those families whose adjusted gross income is less than $ 260K and single folks who make than $ 200K are to be awarded no tax reduction at all.

(That exception covers 10 million or 40% of the total number of pass- throughs. And, pass-throughs garner some 56% of all business income. You should also know that the top 1% income earners receive 70% of all partnership income in the US.)

While the alternative minimum tax (AMT) remains in force for individuals, the concept has been eradicated when it comes to business income. Moreover, those firms that paid AMT may be able to use those funds to refund the taxes that will be due for taxes due between 2018 and 2021 (inclusive) up to 50% of the AMT (100% for tax years 2021 and 2022).

What about those pass-through entities. 20% of the distributions from pass-through entities (LLC, partnerships, S corporations, Schedule C [self-employed) businesses, trusts, and estates) will be not taxed. Only 80% of that income will be subject to individual (or married) tax rates; the persons to which the pass-through income belongs. There are phase-outs, depending upon one's marital status and income, as well as how much wages the firm provided its employees.

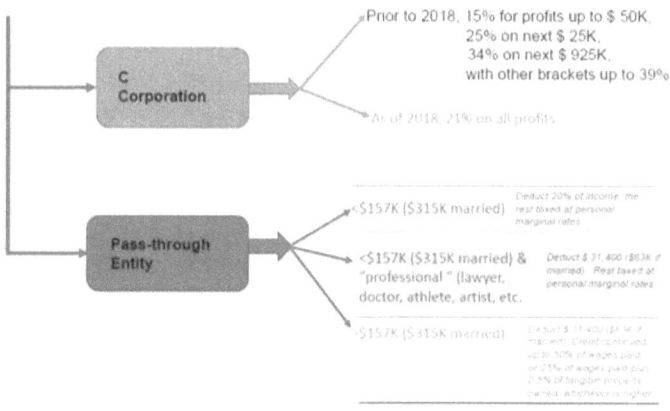

(*This pass-through benefit covers 10 million or 40% of the total number of pass-throughs. And, pass-throughs garner some 56% of all business income. You should also know that the top 1% income-earners receive 70% of all partnership income in the US. But, the pass-through benefits will be attenuated because of the wage cap limiting this tax provision.*)

Active owners (*remember- they don't get the benefit of that reduced tax rate for pass-throughs*) who are in the professional services (lawyers, doctors, accountants, etc.) will probably be paying a 37% tax rate from now on. (This will become clearer when we discuss personal income taxes later on.) Other active owners (such as retailers or manufacturers) will be treated as CEO and investors. As such, 80% of the pass-through income will be taxed at the individual's tax rate.

(By the way, you can bet this will change the way the IRS decides what is reasonable compensation for such firms. It will become standard for reasonable compensation to be at least 30% of the potential pass-through revenue, if not at an even higher level.)

Accounting Rules

Right now, some small businesses are eligible to use "cash accounting". Cash accounting means the firm recognizes income when it is received and expenses when they are paid. Accrual accounting would mean that income is recognized when a client/customer is billed (regardless of when they pay the tab) and expenses are recognized once the bill is received (even if the business has not paid the bill).

The rules for who could cash accounting changed with the new law. It used to be that partnerships (only those with no corporate partner), sole proprietorships, and S entities. Corporations- whether alone or in a partnership can only use cash accounting if they accrue less than $ 5 million in gross receipts. Farms (corporate entities or in partnership with a corporation) need to abandon cash accounting when their gross receipts exceed $ 1 million.

With one big proviso. If a business is selling widgets (products- not services, that requires the firm to amass inventory to handle the demands of the marketplace), the rules for accounting are different. For inventory-based businesses, cash accounting is out once the gross receipts reach $ 1 million. (*There are very specialized exceptions which let the cutoff be $ 10 million, but these are pretty arcane.*)

The new law changes all that. As of now, *Cash Accounting* will be allowable for all entities, as long as annual gross revenue does not exceed $ 25 million.

And, while I said the rules were subject to change when one had inventory, well, the IRS considers firms that undertake long-term contracts kind of have an inventory of sorts. (*For example, many R&D projects involve 3-year terms. That's the sort of inventory-like situation we are discussing here.*) When these relationships exist, the firm must use the *percentage of completion* method to account for income and expenses. Unless, for the past three years, gross receipts did not exceed $10 million a year- then percentage of completion can even be used for projects that have a two-year time frame or less. The proposed law will raise that exception to $ 25 million.

Estate and Trust Taxes

The provisions for Estates and Trusts (as filed on Form 1041) have not changed very much as a result of the new tax law- with two exceptions.

The first involves the Estate Tax exclusion. Now, there is no need to file a form 706 (Estate and Generation Skipping Transfer of Funds) unless the valuation of the estate is $ 11.2 million in 2018 (which be indexed for inflation, a system that used to obtain, but hasn't been used lately). That's more than twice the prior limit of $ 5 million.

Estate Taxes	
≤ $ 2550	10%
> $ 2550 and ≤ $ 9150	$ 255.00, plus 24% over $ 2550
> $ 9150 and ≤ $ 12500	$ 1839.00, plus 35% over $ 9150
> $ 12500	$ 3011.40, plus 37% over $ 12500

And, for those estates and trusts that must file annual tax returns, the tax brackets for estates have been changed. There are four limits- 10%, 24%, 35%, and 37%. Moreover, if the net profits from the trust or estate pass through to beneficiaries, those funds are afforded the 20% pass-through provision discussed in the business section (pass-through entities).

Other Provisions- Colleges

The final bill kept the provision that charged colleges that have "extravagant" investments with an excise tax. The law includes a 1.4% tax on earnings accrued to various investments of private colleges.

But, this provision will not apply to all private colleges. Just those that have amassed endowments that exceed $ 250K per registered student. That attacks some 60 to 70 universities, including Harvard, Princeton, Stanford, and Grinnell.

I can tell you that many of the colleges claim these endowments are critical to maintain funds for salaries, research, and financial aids. Other schools have problems dispensing part of their endowments because donors have stipulated restricted use on some of the funds they receive- and it takes more time to use the funds to comply with those demands.

For example, the last school mentioned above. Grinnell is a teeny school. 1700 undergrads tucked away in Iowa. And, they provide 90% of their students with financial aid, to the tune of $ 50 million a year. But, then, again, Grinnell has a $ 1.6 billion endowment. That's 32 years of the annual scholarship needs. And, this tax will yank something on the order of $ 1.5 million from Grinnell to the US Treasury.

Yeah, you can see that I am still not really crying about this part of the proposed tax provision. But, as I stated above, this provision reflects the bias behind this bill. Most of the affected colleges are considered "liberal". Which makes them cannon fodder for the authors of tax bill. (*You do recall that these passed with not ONE vote from the Democratic party members.*)

The initial versions of the bill included a provision to tax student tuition grants (which primarily affected graduate STEM [science, technology, engineering, and math] programs. That provision, thankfully, has been removed. These potentially affected folks- 65% of US graduate students- can continue to receive these benefits on a tax-free basis.

Chapter 2: Business Interest & Capital Items

Business Interest

Up until the change in the law, businesses could deduct the costs for interest for items that have been financed. That is no longer true. The new law stipulates that only that interest that equals 30% or less of the adjusted taxable income (not counting taxes, depreciation, amortization, and the total amount of interest paid) will be deductible- plus any business interest the entity receives. And, if the entity is a partnership, the rule applies to the entire entity (the one that files an income tax return- not to the individual partners, who will receive their pro-rata share listed on the K-1. (*The K-1 is akin to a W-2 for employees; the K-1 explains how corporate revenue and expenses are allocated to the shareholders.*)

There is a relief valve for smaller enterprises. Entities that have a gross income of $ 25 million or less are entitled to deduct all the interest they pay. The legislation provides that $ 25 million exception because the framers recognized that smaller businesses are less likely to find investors (who buy stock and, therefore, invest capital in the firm). These smaller entities generally must borrow money for their equipment, since they lack access to the stock market.

Oh, and commercial real estate firms also have special rules that make this interest deduction rule less onerous on their continued operation.

Capital and Depreciation

When one buys tangible assets, the value of that asset decreases over time. So, the Internal Revenue Service code lets business account for this decrease using what is called depreciation. Different assets have different useful lives- so the depreciation rules account for the reduction in value over the useful life of the asset. Commercial property is considered to have a 39-year life, residential homes are considered to have a 27.5 y useful life, but computers have a 5-year life.

But, certain property, called "qualified property" can be depreciated over shorter periods than its useful life. "Qualified property" is an item that follows what is called MACRS (modified accelerated cost recovery system); the property has a useful life (aka, recovery period) of 20 years or less. The additional write off is 50% in 2017, 40% in 2018, and 30% in 2019.

The tax law presents new rules that will cover all "qualified property" placed in service between 27 September 2017 and 1 January 2023. These rules allow business to literally write off the costs. 100% of the cost will be able to be expensed immediately. (You did notice this benefit expires after 5 years though, right?)

Moreover, the new law considers qualified property to include non-residential real estate components such as roofing, HVAC (Heating, ventilation, and air conditioning) equipment, fire protection and alarms, as well as security property.

These new rules are separate and apart from Section 179 depreciation. These "sort-of" special depreciation rules that have been in force for almost 6 decades now. Any property that costs $ 1KK or less can be "expensed" in the calendar year of purchase. Up to $ 2.5 million of capital items can be handled this way- the only limitation is the amount of profits the firm has. (It is impossible to create "negative" income- using Section 179 depreciation to reduce one's profits to below zero. On top of this requirement, there is a $ 25K sport utility vehicle limitation. But, all three numbers (the $ 1 KK, the $ 2.5KK, and the $ 25K limits) will be subject to inflation after 2018.

Luxury Automobile Depreciation	Cars Acquired before 28 Sept 2017, placed in service in CY 2018	Cars Acquired after 27 Sept 2017, placed in service in CY 2018
Year 1	$ 16,400	$ 18,000
Year 2	$ 16,400	$ 16,000
Year 3	$ 9,600	
Succeeding years	$ 5,760	

One of the biggest changes PL115-97 made is to the limits of car depreciation- they are greatly increased. The new limits are $ 10K for the first year of car ownership (which is about 3X as high as obtained before the law's enactment), a limit of $ 16K for year 2, which decreased to $ 9600 for year three. Subsequent year's depreciation limits are set at $ 5760. (*Prior to this change in the law, many of our clients needed 6 years to depreciate a moderate priced vehicle [$ 35K]. Now, this will only take 3 years! But, there's a new wrinkle for cars that we discuss immediately below*)

Section 1031 Exchanges

Most taxpayers assumed Section 1031 exchanges were exclusively reserved for real estate sales, because they didn't realize that many of the transactions they effected fell under this provision. Under a Section 1031 exchange, the seller identified a property that can be bought that is "similar" [in function, not necessarily in size or location]; in so doing, any capital gains that accrued on the sale of the property were extended until a subsequent property were sold and not exchanged. In essence, the basis of the property is rolled into basis of the new property, which means the IRS doesn't get to collect taxes for a while (until there is no longer a 1031 exchange made upon the property sale).

But, despite the fact that most taxpayers thought 1031 exchanges only applied to reals estate, there were a slew of items that one routinely sold and replaced with new items that were covered by this exception.

No- not stocks, bonds, or partnership shares. (In other words, things that are held primarily to promote a sale of the item in the future to generate a gain.) Did you realize that this exception covered the trading in of a business vehicle? When you sold your 2014 Glitzmobile that you bought for $ 30,000, depreciated in value down to $19,000 and bought a 2018 Sportsmobile for $ 40,000 (the dealer credited your old car at $ 20,000 of the new car price), you really were effecting a 1031 exchange. You really made a $ 1,000 profit on the sale of the car- but you rolled that basis into the Sportsmobile. Which would not create a taxable event until you stopped trading in your old car for a new one. (This exchange rule applied not only to real estate and vehicles, but to planes, collectibles, and equipment.)

Except, the new law stipulates that 1031 exchanges will only be allowed for real property from now on. So, now, instead of trading in your car, you will have to sell it directly (or track the sales price you obtain). Because business will have to complete Form 4797, denoting the depreciated value and sales value of the car. And, taxes will be due on the gains between the sale price and the depreciated value of the vehicle (or plane, collectible, etc.)

So, from now on- don't trade in your business vehicle. Sell it first! You will generally get more money for it than you would from a car dealer, but since you've probably depreciated it anyway (so it is technically worthless), you can use some of those gains to pay for the taxes on your disposition of the vehicle.

Chapter 3. Business Travel, Meals, and Entertainment

Up until the enactment of PL115-97, business could deduct the costs of a fair amount of entertainment (including golfing) and meals. Those regulations are very different now.

We couldn't deduct the full cost of our entertainment expenses in 2017 and before; only 50% of what we spent was deductible against our profits. That same deductibility applies to meals, unless those meals were proffered to our employees as a means to have them keep working (like overtime or working through lunches). The other half of the expense was not deductible against one's profits.

Except the new law outlaws ALL entertainment expenses. No amusement or recreational activities or membership dues related to these activities or for social purposes. No transportation fringe benefits and provisions for the deductibility of on-premises gyms.

Moreover, if the firm were a non-profit entity, the cost such activities will now be taxable to the non-profit!

Although not entertainment, this section also disallowed the deduction of qualified transportation expenses for employees, nor can commutation costs between an employee's residence and the place of employment be deductible. (There is a provision to expense transportation costs when those costs are necessary for the safety of the employee.)

Employee meals

Entertainment-Related

What is the expense?	2017 Rules	2018 and beyond
Sporting Tickets	50% of Ticket's Face Value is deductible	0 deductiblity
	100% for charitable sports events	0 deductibility
	80% of right to purchase educational facility's sports events	0 deductibility
	50% of sport events transportation and parking	0 deductibility
Entertainment-related meals	50% deductible	If no business conducted- 0 deductibility (which means night clubs, theaters, country clubs, sports)
Club memberships	0 deductibility for club dues; 50% of club expenses related to active trade or business	0 deductibility

What about those employee meals? The ones we bought for our employees when, instead of going home at 5, they kept working until 8:30, 9:30, or even 11 PM?

Up until the signing of this new law, employers were able to provide meals for their staff if they worked through lunch or through dinner, or worked hours of overtime. The concept was that employers provided these meals so their staff wouldn't leave the premises; and, as such, the tax code allowed the employer to deduct 100% of the costs for such meals.

Except the new law stipulates that the employer may only deduct ½ the cost of those meals. In other words, these meals will have the same deduction rate as the cost for any other meal the company wishes to deduct.

Oh, wait. It gets worse. As of 1 January 2026, these meals will NOT be deductible at all. The employer will have to eat the entire cost of such provided meals.

Besides entertainment and employee meals, meals in general now are covered by different regulations.

When we or our employees travel on business, the costs for airfare, train fare, bus fare, even mileage are fully deductible. As are hotel costs and incidentals (like the purchase of a newspaper). And, the costs for the meals that we purchase when we are traveling are also deductible.

The law still lets us deduct the meals when we are traveling to go to a meeting or to visit a customer. (That means if one leaves the day before the meeting to ensure that

Also unchanged are the deductibility for the day(s) of travel to and from the destination are considered part. (You should now that many folks never avail themselves of those "extra" days of travel; that practice stems from the desire to spend as much time with our kids as possible, even if it meant one had to fly the midnight special.) And, each day of one's business trip is deductible as long as FOUR (4) hours of business is conducted per day. (That rule does not include the travel days.)

That brings up a key point, too. If you have a business meeting on Friday and another one on Monday, then the weekend is considered part of the business trip. [I have used this trick often- especially if I brought my kid(s) along for the fun.]

As a matter of course the following items are 100% deductible- both under the old regime and the new tax law.

Deductible Travel Expenses (100%)

Public transportation- airfare, subway, trolley, bus, train
Mileage should you elect to drive to the destination,
    as well mileage to and from the bus/train/air terminals
Taxi- conventional, Lyft, or Uber.
Accommodations- hotel, AirBnB, Vrbo
Registration fees for the meeting (including any supplies)
Rental car, gas, and related fees
Parking- at the transportation hub or at the destination
Tolls
Valet, baggage handling, tips

Travel-Related

What is the expense?	2017 Rules	2018 and beyond
Meals during business travels	50% deductible	50% deductible
Meals at Conference, Seminar, Business League event	50% deductible	50% deductible
Meals included in Charitable Sports Package	100% deductible	50% deductible

But, what about the meals when we travel? While the rules say they are 100% business related, the law also limits the deductibility of those expenses to 50% of the total. (This same percentage deduction obtained under the old rules.) And, the cost of meals means the tip you leave the staff, too. Tips one provides wait staff is NOT to be included under the above list mentioning tips. These are food related; as such, they are also limited to the 50% deduction rules.

We can't get carried away, either. You can't deduct golfing fees while you are away. It makes no difference if we went by ourselves, with a client, with a partner, with an employee, or with a prospect.

Nor can spa expenses (pedicures or manicures) appear, either. Nor can we deduct movies (even if you go to one of those hotels that has pay-per-view- and it's not educational if you seek out one starring or directed by Stormy Daniels). Which should make it clear that a Broadway (or other theater) show is also off the list for deductions. Yup, you guessed it- no concerts, either.

And, the costs to attend the games of my beloved Phillies (or any other sports event)- even as I take a client with me- nope. They are now the overhead expenses for our firm- or my personal expenses.

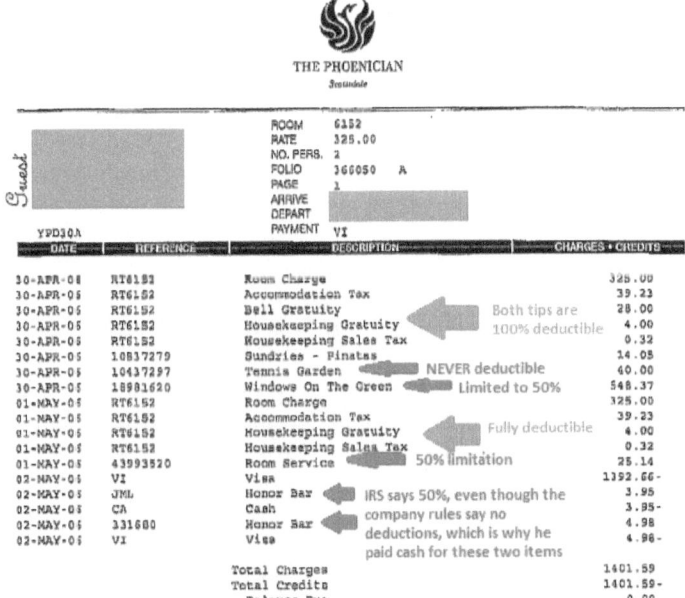

Here's a special caveat, since I've had clients try this in the past. Do NOT consider charging your room service or hotel meals to the hotel bill. Oh, sure, you can charge them to make it easier to handle your bill. But those costs MUST be delineated and separated from the accommodation charge. Because accommodations are fully deductible, but meals are limited to 50%. And, you can bet the IRS will be very carefully examining (ok, via a paper audit) those charges.

Entertainment

Entertainment-Related

What is the expense?	2017 Rules	2018 and beyond
Sporting Tickets	50% of Ticket's Face Value is deductible	0 deductiblity
	100% for charitable sports events	0 deductibility
	80% of right to purchase educational facility's sports events	0 deductibility
	50% of sport events transportation and parking	0 deductibility
Entertainment-related meals	50% deductible	If no business conducted- 0 deductibility (which means night clubs, theaters, country clubs, sports)
Club memberships	0 deductibility for club dues; 50% of club expenses related to active trade or business	0 deductibility

Most of you know that entertainment expenses under the old laws were only 50% deductible. Just like meals, unless the meals are provided to one's employees as a means to have them keep working (like overtime or working through lunches). The other half of the expense was not deductible against one's profits.

Except the new law outlaws ALL entertainment expenses. No amusement or recreational activities or membership dues related to these activities or for social purposes. No transportation fringe benefits and no on-premises gyms.

And, if this were a non-profit entity, these sorts of activities will now be taxable to the non-profit!

Although not entertainment, this section also disallows the deduction of qualified transportation expenses for employees (except when necessary for the safety of the employee) or to assist in commutation costs between an employee's residence and the place of employment.

Of course, this law also affected how we meet with clients- and where. If we meet in a night club or theater, the law stipulates those as entertainment- and not client-related. As such, they are non-deductible business expenses. (If the night club were to separate out the cost of admission (or cover charge) and charges for food separately, the rules are different. See the next paragraph.)

But, if we take a client to the Phillies ball game, the rules are a little different. The cost of the ticket- that's on us or our company (not deductible). But, the cost of a vegetarian hamburger and/or a beer, then that's a client-based meal- for which half is deductible on our taxes.

Clients-Meal Related

What is the expense?	2017 Rules	2018 and beyond
Client Business Meals	50% deductible, if taxpayer present	50% deductible, if taxpayer is present AND business is transacted
Travel to/from Client Business Meal	100% deductible	100% deductible
Meal Expenses Sold to client or customer (or reimbursed)	100% deductible	100% deductible
Food offered to the public for free (e.g., during a seminar)	100% deductible	100% deductible

But, if we meet a client at a restaurant, that meal is deductible (50%)- but we must prove that business was transacted. Otherwise, the law deems the meal to be an entertainment event and not deductible. And, if it is not deductible as a meal, then the travel to and/or from that meal is not a deductible expense.

Chapter 4. Miscellaneous Tax Changes

Net Operating Losses

It happens. Sometimes a firm generates less revenue that it's expenses. And, when that happens, the firm incurs a loss. In the past, the IRS code permitted the firm to carry back that loss to the previous two years. To do that, the firm must submit an amended tax return for those years. That also means the firm has agreed to extend the Audit Statute of Limitations- because that period is six (6) years from the date of filing (an amended return creates a new date of filing). Which is why many firms elected to carry the tax loss forward for the next 20 years, until the loss had been extinguished. (This is akin to individual taxpayers dealing with a big stock loss- except that doesn't get carried backward, just forward, with a maximum capital loss of $ 3K a year allowed.)

The new rules will no longer let losses incurred in CY 2018 or later to be carried back. Only the carryforward rules will be allowed. Moreover, there is a limitation to the carryforward provision. The carryforward is limited to the lesser of NOL (net operating loss) carryover or 80% of the entity's pre-NOL deductible taxable income. (This is called the 80% limitation rule).

Pass-through entities have special rules, too. If the firm incurs a loss, then the 20% deduction of pass-through income obviously has no bearing. (After all, the reduction applies only to positive income; 20% of zero is still zero.) But, the carryforward years are also complicated.

Let's use an example that Bantam LLC incurred a $ 20,000 loss in 2018, but generated $ 120,000 in profits for 2019. As stated, there is no 20% deduction for 2018. But, for 2019, the firm can only get a 20% reduction to $ 100,000 [2019's profit of $ 120K less the less the loss carry-forward of $ 20K for 2018].

Excessive compensation

Did you know that when a public entity pays its top five employees (by compensation, not title) more than $ 1 million, the portion that exceeded $ 1 million was not deductible by the company? Which is why so many firms have been providing stock incentives and other commissions to those folks- to get around the limitation.

FY 2011	Microsoft	Apple	
Gross Revenue	69,943	108,249	1000s
Net Income	23,150	25,992	1000s
Employees	90,000	63,300	
Executive compensation	53,320	148,425	1000s
Executive/Starting Pay Ratio	123	689	
Executive/Mid-career Pay Ratio	84	265	

Notice the pay ratios between executives and employees[/caption]

Notice the pay ratios between executives and employees, provided by example, above. That's not going to fly anymore. The bill recognizes that companies switched from cash compensation to stock options and other pay-for-performance options. And, then the executives manipulate the firm's short-term results to ensure they obtain those incentives. The executives may still manipulate the numbers, but any compensation so received would still be part and parcel of that $ 1 million threshold- even if it is a "stock" bonus.

Non-profit entity executives were also subject to the $ 1 million threshold. Now, any such compensation to the five highest paid executives in excess of $ 1 million will be subject to a 20% excise tax. (Yes, that means non-profits will owe some taxes.)

Lobbying

Until the law was pass, the law did not allow businesses to deduct the costs of lobbying. (*You may now realize why so many of these lobbying firms want to be considered to be "public relations" entities; by not registering as "lobbyists"*, the provisions didn't apply to them.)

However, there was an exception. The costs incurred to lobby a local government entity were allowed to be deductible under the old law. When businesses lobby our local governments, the IRS was required to accept those costs as deductible.

That exception evaporates under the new law. So, no lobbying costs are deductible.

Carried Interest

The law made no real changes to the carried interest provisions. These gains are treated as capital gains with a maximum tax rate of 23.8%, if they are held for three years. Otherwise, they would be taxed at the marginal tax rate that obtains (which could be as high as 37%). But, don't worry, the firms that generate such funds ensure that they are always considered long-term capital gains.

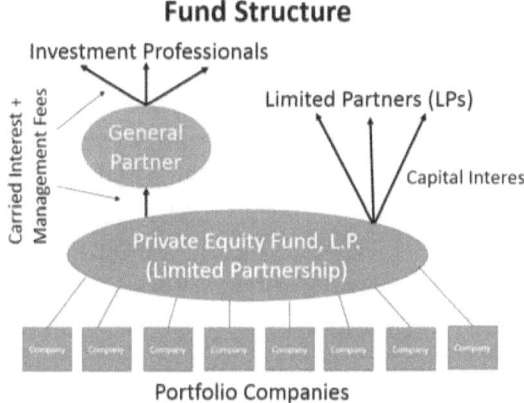

Oh, and these benefits apply even if they had a cashless contribution (i.e., none of their money was involved in the transaction; so it's interest garnered on zero!) in the investment (or used a "waiver of management fee") to justify this tax preference.

Patents

```
            Canadian Intellectual    Office de la propriété
            Property Office          intellectuelle du Canada                  Canadä
            An Agency of             Un organisme
            Industry Canada          d'Industrie Canada
Home > CIPO > Patent Summary
Canadian Patents Database

Patent Summary

(12) Patent:                        (11) CA 1042814

(21) Application Number:            200059

(54) English Title:                 HEMO DIALYZER SYSTEM EMPLOYING TWO DIALYSATE
                                    SOLUTIONS

(54) French Title:                  HEMODIALYSEUR A DOUBLE DIALYSAT

Patent Details

(52) Canadian Patent
Classification (CPC):               102/15

(51) International Patent           A61M 1/16 (2006.01)
Classification (IPC):               A61M 1/03 (1980.01)

(72) Inventors (Country):
                                    ACKERMAN, ROY A. (Not Available)
```

The provision on patents is similar to that of carried interest. Prior to the new law, when we sold a patent (or were paid for their value), the gains (the compensation received) were considered to be a long-term capital gain. (That was true as long as we did not sell the patent the first year we obtained it- under the old provisions, that gain was considered to be a short-term capital gain.) There were provisions in the various drafts to remove this capability (and denote the gains as ordinary income) - but like the carried interest provisions, these stay in force.

Credits

It is easier to describe what the new law has taken away.

Under the old law, employers could provide a child care credit towards the care of employee's offspring. It had been limited to 25% of the costs- up to $

150,000. But, as of 2018, this credit is no longer available to employers.

Also, when a business rehabilitated an historic building, the old tax code provided special tax provisions. The government considered this to be a valuable public service, and, therefore, used the tax code to provide some benefit to the business for the costs incurred. This provision has been removed; there is no rehabilitation credit for historic buildings.

The government also decided that it will no longer provide a credit for a business to make its facilities accessible for the disabled. (Please note that this credit has been around for a long time. By now, most of the firms that had occupied buildings that lacked such capability should have modified their structures to make them more accessible. So, the loss of the credit is not a major political decision, but more a recognition that it was no longer necessary.)

The work opportunity credit had provided incentives for businesses to hire veterans, citizens receiving financial assistance from the government (TANF- tax assistance for needy families, SNAP- supplemental nutrition assistance program [food stamps], the long term unemployed, etc.) and other targeted groups. The credit ranged from 25% of wages to 40%, with a maximum limit per individual. This credit expires at the end of next year.

Moreover, any unused business credit- for any reason- can no longer be carried forward or backward. (It's now 'use it or lose it'.)

Chapter 5: Other Financial Considerations

Municipal Bonds

Some localities offer what is termed Private Activity Bonds- bonds that are sold to help (or induce) local firms stay in their locations and/or upgrade their facilities. (Some bonds are also offered to help firms decide to relocate to the municipality in question.) Taxpayers who purchased such bonds (in essence, they funded the activity) will no longer be able to deduct the interest received on these bonds as tax-free; that interest will now be taxable. In particular, those public stadiums that localities have been financing? That interest payment will now be taxable.

Partnership Terminations

Termination of a partnership has heretofore been defined as when the business ceases to be functional or there is a sale of 50% or more (in a given year) of the partnerships' capital and/or profit interests. The latter reason is called a technical termination.

Under the proposed law, technical terminations would no longer be mandated. The partnership can still be considered to be ongoing and patent.

Municipal Bonds

Some localities offer what is termed Private Activity Bonds- bonds that are sold to help (or induce) local firms stay in their locations and/or upgrade their facilities. (Some bonds are also offered to help firms decide to relocate to the municipality in question.) Taxpayers who purchased such bonds (in essence, they funded the activity) will no longer be able to deduct the interest received on these bonds as tax-free; that interest will now be taxable. In particular, those public stadiums that localities have been financing? That interest payment will now be taxable.

Foreign Income

Right now, foreign income earned by a foreign subsidiary of an American firm is not taxed until the profits are returned to the American firm. And, the tax on that income is subject to a reduction to the US taxes due, so as to reflect the foreign taxes the firm paid on said income before it was repatriated.

Now, under the newly enacted law, if the foreign entity is more than 10% owned by the US corporation, that repatriated income would be totally exempt from US taxes.

There's a repatriation provision, too. Foreign entities will now be responsible to pay the IRS a 20% excise tax on subsidiary payments made for goods or services rendered to a foreign affiliate. Up to now, this is how folks like Apple (among many other companies) have hidden their taxable transactions from the IRS (in plain sight, of course).

Under this new proviso. those "royalties" that tech firms and big pharma "pay" their subsidiaries to shelter the profits from taxation will now be subject to this 20% levy. Not quite as good as my plan- but it's better than a poke in the eye.

There's yet another provision that covers taxation of foreign income. Although it's officially called GILTI (pun intended? Global Intangible Low-Taxed Income), it's not just directed to licensing and royalties (such as those derived from patents). This is actually a tax on "excess foreign profit", where a firm's overseas tax bill is below a threshold level. Through 2025, this means corporations will be taxed at approximately 10.5% on that income (rising after that to about 13%). But, pass-through entities may not be able to use that special 10.5% rate- but the rate of the individual stockholder or partner (in other words, as high as 37%).

Yet another provision hits up FDIT (foreign derived intangible income) for a rate of about 13.1% for domestic corporations. Pass-throughs also would be taxed at the marginal rate of the individual stockholder (or partner).

(Don't feel too bad for these entities. I am betting they will be forming C Corporations (conventional

corporations) to maintain their foreign assets. That will afford them the 10.5% tax rate.)

Banks

Not surprisingly, banks are going to do very well under this new program. They'll be raking in the money subject to the 21% tax rate. Until now, they paid significantly higher rates than the rest of US businesses. Now, they'll probably save more than $ 12 billion (assuming they do as well/badly as they had in 2016). As a matter of fact, just the 5 largest banks will have more than $ 11 billion added to their treasuries under this law.)

Not even the change in interest deductibility will hurt them! Since banks rake in far more interest payments than they shell out, the 30% limitation on deductible interest (based upon cash flow) won't exacerbate their new tax situation.

The biggest hit (for the biggest banks) will be the removed deduction of FDIC (Federal Deposit Insurance Corporation) payments, when the bank's assets exceed $ 50 billion.

Base Erosion

This is a recognition that the world is adopting a base erosion program to fully obtain taxes on income that heretofore was not considered to be subject to that nations' taxes.

This provision now taxes what is termed Part F income from foreign subsidiaries, regardless of whether those funds are repatriated or not. If the entity exceeded the total of the Federal short-term rate plus 7% on the basis of depreciable tangible property (this is called its asset base), then that excess will be taxed at the appropriate rate (the existing tax bracket) for the corporation.

As discussed above, there also will be that excise tax charged to funds that an American firm provides a related foreign corporation (other than interest) that are considered costs of goods sold or are part of a depreciable or amortization asset would be subject to an excise tax of 20%.

Regarding business credits, the R&D credit is preserved in the Senate version of the bill, as is the low-income housing credit (to induce business to create more residences for those at the lower end of the income spectrum).

Excise Taxes on Alcohol

I couldn't figure out which liquor firm bought this benefit (*I'm sure it wasn't craft breweries- more on that below; the concept of helping small breweries was proposed by Senator Ron Wyden (D-OR), but Senator Rob Portman (R-OH) spliced this bigger deal into the tax package*), but it's pretty substantial. First, a little history. Breweries paid $ 7 in excise taxes per barrel (up to 60,000 barrels), but the big guys paid $ 18 a barrel (up to 6 million of them). No more. Now, the taxes are $ 3.50 and $ 16, respectively.

But, liquor taxes also got creamed. Until now, the tax was $ 13.50 a gallon. Now, for the first 100,000 gallons (produced or imported), that rate drops to $ 2.70.

Wine taxes are also cut (but only until 1 January 2020). But, it's a more difficult discussion, since the wine industry gets taxed based on the alcohol content of the wine. Champagne, which had a special tax of $ 3.15, will now be taxed like it's still wine. Until now, wine under 14% alcohol accrued a tax of $ 1.07. But, the new law makes the tax volume dependent (and raised the alcohol limit to 16%): The first 30,000 gallons accrues a $ 1 per gallon tax, which drops to 90 cents for the next 100,000 gallons. Which then drops to all of $0.535 on the next 620,000 gallons. Also, wine with a high alcohol content (>21%) will see their taxes drop from $3.15 a gallon down to the rates for liquor (above).

By the way, don't expect those $4.2 billion in tax savings to show up in your pocket. (*Note further that the total amount of savings accruing to the small breweries and wineries will reap all of $80 million. The rest goes to the "big boys" of the business.*) The price for wine, beer, and alcohol will simply swell to absorb the tax savings. (*So much for trickle down.*)

Oil Spills

I know- you can look through the entire tax document (PL115-97) and not find one mention about this oil spill "tax".

That's because it wasn't included in this law. So, the excise tax (Section 4611) imposed on crude oil delivered to an American refinery, finished petroleum products that reach American shores (for use, consumption, or even warehousing), or domestically produced crude oil is no more.

This means importers and/or refinery operators will no longer be required to provide the IRS 9 cents in excise taxes per barrel. what was that money for? To cover our costs to clean up after the firms that provided an oil spill- like BP, Exxon, and a slew of other firms.

Yes, this tax (average collections were $500 million a year) was imposed right before we had to deal with the Exxon Valdez spill (1989). Way back in 1986. And, it didn't just cover the costs of oil spills- but is provided to ensure pipeline safety. (Hmm. Remember that South Dakota pipeline spill late last year?)

Whew. Up to this line, we've used up 4023 words (plus pictures) to cover the business provisions of PL 115-97. 3580 (plus a preamble of 783 words) to discuss the personal tax provisions. 8386 words in all. Good thing words are cheap- this tax bill ain't!

We can bet that the politicians will be looking at non-defense spending to find a way to fund the $ 1.5 trillion benefit provided businesses in this new tax bill.

Tax Collections

Ah, yes. The truth- and the dangers- are now becoming obvious.

Politicians were desperate to provide a benefit to their benefactors. So, they lowered the corporate tax rates to a ridiculously low 21%. Even though most corporations never paid the much bandied about 35% rate. (*Only professional corporations and small businesses got stuck with that tax rate. The larger businesses have always found ways to hide- and will probably continue to do so- their profits from the tax man.*)

Politicians also promised wage increases would result from the lowered corporate tax rates. That corporations would benevolently provide those increases as a result of the tax cuts. Except, they don't exist.

Instead those tax cuts are being used to increase executive pay, to allow stock buybacks, and to acquire competitors.

Right now, inflation in the US, while under control, is the highest it has been in a very long time. Since the Great Recession. As you can see in the graph below, it's increasing way over the expected rates. Given that wages are not increasing, it means workers have much less disposable cash- because inflation is eating away at the little they are paid.

Which means it will be much harder for the Federal Reserve to apply its magic as the situation worsens. And, the Feds problem is compounded by an important factor- the effect of the tax cuts.

You see, the lower tax rates have cut into the collections of funds the U.S. Treasury collects to fund the government. This past month, the IRS collected 33% less from corporate taxes than it did exactly 1 year ago. Yes, it's true that corporate taxes never accounted *(in the last three decades or so)* for the bulk of the US revenue *(precipitously dropping from 30% of treasury collections in the late 1950's)*- to some 9% of total taxes collected by the IRS. But, that means- if all else were equal- revenue that the government needs to pay its bill dropped by 3% compared to last year.

But, it's not the only drop. Payroll taxes dropped by 5%. And payroll taxes account for about 40% of the total US collections. Which means there's an additional overall hit to the Treasury of about another 2%.

And, estimated taxes- the taxes paid by unincorporated businesses, and the self-employed or folks who earn significant revenue from non-payroll sources- dropped by 7%.

Yup, the IRS is now collecting about 8% less money than it did last year. And, last year we had a big deficit- and contributed virtually nothing to maintain (*forget about improving*) our infrastructure.

The good thing is that the government is spending less money than last year. About 9% less, now that we no longer have those unfunded liabilities (*the War in Iraq and Afghanistan that were prosecuted primarily off-budget*). But, the federal deficit is still swelling. For the first nine months of FY 2018 *(remember that the federal budget runs from October to October)*, the deficit was about $ 607 billion- about 1/6 larger than it was for the same 9 months of FY 2017.

One can only hope that the great increase in tax collections collected from corporate coffers promised by the politicians will arrive. Soon.

Transfer Pricing

Some folks may consider this a case about tax havens, others about how companies manipulate expenses between domestic and overseas operations. Either way, it's a big win for the IRS.

> 145 T.C. No. 3
>
> UNITED STATES TAX COURT
>
> ALTERA CORPORATION AND SUBSIDIARIES, Petitioner v.
> COMMISSIONER OF INTERNAL REVENUE, Respondent
>
> Docket Nos. 6253-12, 9963-12. Filed July 27, 2015.
>
> In Xilinx, Inc. v. Commissioner, 125 T.C. 37 (2005), aff'd, 598 F.3d 1191 (9th Cir. 2010), we held that, under the 1995 cost-sharing regulations, controlled entities entering into qualified cost-sharing agreements (QCSAs) need not share stock-based compensation (SBC) costs because parties operating at arm's length would not do so. In 2003 Treasury issued sec. 1.482-7(d)(2), Income Tax Regs. (final rule). The final rule requires controlled parties entering into QCSAs to share SBC costs.
>
> P is an affiliated group of corporations that filed consolidated returns for the years in issue. A-US, the parent company, is a Delaware corporation, and A-I, a subsidiary of A-US, is a Cayman Islands corporation. A-US and A-I entered into a QCSA. During its 2004-07 taxable years A-US granted SBC to its employees. A-US did not share the SBC costs with A-I. R determined deficiencies based on I.R.C. sec. 482 allocations R made pursuant to the final rule.

The original decision, favoring Altera over the IRS

We have to go back a little way. It seems the Tax Court (*you know, one of those administrative entities that ends up deciding most of the cases in the US- faster than the courts do*) rendered a decision in favor of Altera Corporation (*now a subsidiary of Intel*). Altera wasn't happy with the way the IRS ruled on its expense allocations between US and foreign operations. So, they fought the IRS in Tax

Court. And, the Court's decision, 145 TC, Number 3, way back in 2015, basically invalidated Section 482 (of the tax code). Under 26CFR Section 1.482-7A(d)(2), related entities were required to share the costs of employee stock compensation (*to render the arranged as qualified cost-sharing*). The 15-judge panel sided with Altera that the IRS regulations were arbitrary and capricious.

Somehow, the IRS appealed to the 9th Circuit of the US. That court ruled that the IRS was neither arbitrary nor capricious and was in total compliance with the Administrative Procedure Act. Which means the IRS' decisions are the law of the land in this case. Basically, the "arm's length standard", whereby internal corporate transactions must be analyzed in comparison to what independent (*as opposed to wholly-owned subsidiaries*) would make is the standard.

UNITED STATES COURT OF APPEALS
FOR THE NINTH CIRCUIT

ALTERA CORPORATION & SUBSIDIARIES, Petitioner-Appellee. v. COMMISSIONER OF INTERNAL REVENUE, Respondent-Appellant.	Nos. 16-70496 16-70497 Tax Ct. Nos. 6253-12 9963-12 OPINION

Appeal from a Decision of the
United States Tax Court

Argued and Submitted October 11, 2017
San Francisco, California

Filed July 24, 2018

Before: Sidney R. Thomas, Chief Judge, and Stephen Reinhardt* and Kathleen M. O'Malley** Circuit Judges.

Opinion by Chief Judge Thomas;
Dissent by Judge O'Malley

Here's the crux of the issue. Independent companies never would consider any stock-based compensation as a cost-sharing item among two firms. So, that means that there are no "comparable" independent deals with which to compare the concept- so the IRS was free to develop its own rational split of the costs, relative to the income generated.

(We also must consider that the most "flagrant" cases that apply under Section 482 are stock-based compensation splits and the fairy-tale that intellectual property is that of the overseas subsidiary. This is how Intel and Apple have avoided their true income tax liability for decades. They are not alone- this is the tax dodge used by most technology and pharmaceutical houses- those firms that rely heavily on patent rights.

This has been the practice for decades. Firms claim they pay $ XYZ in federal income tax to their stockholders, and lower the dividend payments they make to accommodate the cash needs of these "tax payments". But, you see these are "provisions for income taxes"- that amount doesn't reflect how the firms manipulate their REAL books (the ones they don't share with stockholders) to appropriate intellectual property and stock-based compensation. Then, that "tax benefit" is accounted for as a "contribution to capital".)

The Logic behind Transfer Pricing

- Where tax rates are different between the countries, there is a strong incentive to shift income to a lower tax country and deductions to a higher tax country so that
- the overall tax effect is minimized.

It is true that US companies are allowed to shift profits to an "offshore" subsidiary to avoid taxes. They are also allowed to identify and shift the costs between such entities. But, the IRS regulations stipulate that more of the costs must be transferred to the subsidiary, and, therefore, wouldn't be deducted under US law. This concept is called "transfer pricing"- and the IRS rarely won cases in such matters.

A Bona-fide Case of Transfer Pricing

(Until the new tax law was enacted last year, the goal of every US company with overseas subsidiaries was to shift as much of its profits overseas and secure as many of the deductions domestically, to ensure that their taxes- which could be as high as 35% [but never were]- would be minimal. The new law, which stipulates a maximum corporate rate of 21%, provides a 13.125% rate on foreign income from goods and services using patents and other technology.)

This may not be settled. It is entirely possible that Intel will now appeal. Or that the US Chamber of Commerce will look for relief from the Supreme Court. *(Amazon had also filed an amicus brief to the 9th Circuit, in support of the Tax Court position.)*

But, for now, the IRS interpretation is the law of the land.

Chapter 6. Pass-Through Provisions

This is an entirely new provision that applies to pass-through entities (including trusts and estates). Partnerships, sole proprietorships, S corporations, and LLC's are among such entities. Under the new law, the pass-through income will receive a 20% deduction. This means that only 80% of the pass-through income will be taxed (subject to wage limits and a few other exceptions). *(NOTE: 100% of the income- regardless of the 20% pass-through exemption is still subject to the self-employment [Medicare and Social Security] taxes.)*

The entire basis of this provision is detailed under Section 199A, as passed on 22 December 2017, and then amended on 23 March 2018 (retroactively to the start of CY 2018). This provision holds for CY 2018 through CY 2025, when it expires.

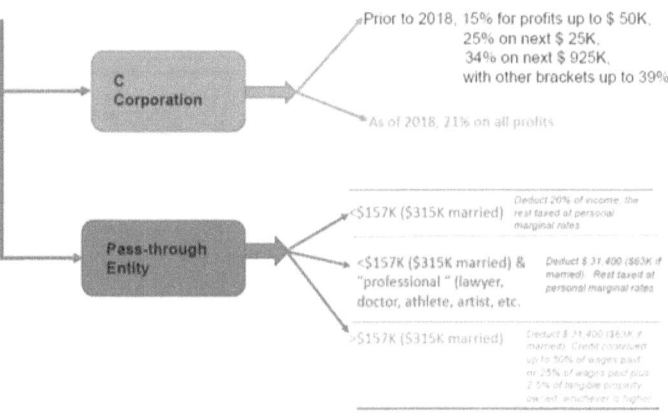

The provision deals specifically with the following business entities:

1. Sole proprietorship
2. Rental Income
3. Partnership
4. Publicly Traded Partnerships (PTP)
5. S Corporations
6. Trusts
7. REIT (real estate investment trusts)
8. Estates

9. LLC's (and choice of operation EXCEPT a C Corporation)

In addition, there is a maximum taxable income (threshold amount) which is dependent upon the sort of trade or activity of the business involved. And, that threshold, in many cases, gets extended (upward) based upon the amount of W-2 wages paid by the entity and/or the unadjusted basis of qualified business property held.

The provision affords the pass-through recipient to deduct the lesser of the 20% of business profits (taxable income) or 20% of the excess taxable income over the net capital gain of the taxpayer for the tax year in question.

To explain this provision, it is important to provide a few examples. The first key question is what is the QBI- the qualified business income (net amount of qualified items of income, gain, deduction, and loss with respect to a specific qualified trade or business). Then, we must know what the individual's *combined* qualified REIT dividends (yes, combined- if any). We also need to determine if there is any qualified PTP income. Finally, we need to know the individuals' net capital gain, which gets subtracted from the 20% of QBI, should there be a capital gain.

How does one handle losses from pass-through entities?

Now, if the QBI (qualified business income) from all entities is negative, or the REIT (real estate investment trusts) dividends and PTP (pass-through partnerships) income is below zero, there is a provision for loss carryovers. Notice that there two situations (QBI AND REIT/PTP) are separate from one another when considering if there is a loss carryover- and each one is separate from the other.

This means, should the firm produce a loss, the taxpayer receives no benefit for that tax year. (Under the prior laws, taxpayers got to reduce their income by the amount of the entire pass-through loss.),

It gets "better". The law provides that the loss gets carried over to the next tax year- which means the loss lowers the 20% benefit one can receive that year! As an example, this means if a firm lost $ 20K in 2018, and produced a profit of $ 120K in 2019, there is a greatly diminished pass-through benefit. Since 20% of zero is zero (for CY 2018), and in 2019, the $ 120K is reduced by $ 20K (the 2018 tax loss carryforward), there is only a 20% special deduction on $ 100K ($120K- $20K loss carryforward).

Each entity is considered separately and then aggregated

Now, considering that there are no losses to consider, we must determine if the threshold for QBI income has been met. If it has, then the limitation is affected by the greater of 50% of W-2 wages or 25% of W-2 wages PLUS 2.5% of unadjusted basis for qualified property. Partnership guaranteed payments or the "reasonable compensation" required to be paid to executives (owners) of S corporations do not apply for the W-2 wages computed above.

So, what are the threshold amounts? For single taxpayers or for married folks filing separately [MFS], the threshold limit is $ 157,500 ($ 315,000 for those folks filing jointly)- for CY 2018. Subsequent years will be subject to a cost-of-living adjustment.

The 20% deduction against income phases out completely for individual (or MFS [married, filing separately]) incomes of $ 207,500 or $ 415,000 for those filing jointly.

And, then, there's another provision that limits the utility of the provision. Firms that provide professional services (lawyers, doctors, accountants, artists, athletes, etc.) have no ability to benefit from the 20% pass-through exemptions when their (personal) gross adjusted incomes exceed the thresholds- despite any W-2 wages or qualified capital investments. (These are the means by which other firms get to extend their thresholds higher.) That is because the government deems these entities to rely on the skill or reputation of 1 or more employees and are, therefore, held to the strictest threshold levels.

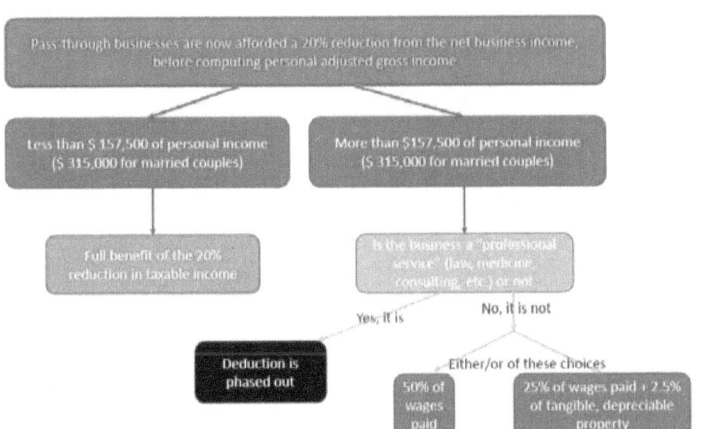

Section Two: Personal Tax Issues

Section Two. Personal Income Taxes

Chapter 7. Tax Rates & Exemptions

So, the first item is a "simplification of individual income tax rates". The original idea propounded in the House bill was to axe the existing 7 tax brackets down to four. But, the Senate prevailed and the final version retains 7 tax brackets, but these rates are at vastly different income levels than prevailed previously, along with different marginal tax rates.

Marginal Tax Rate	Married Filing Jointly		Single		Head of Household	
10%	≤ $19050		≤$9525		≤$13600	
12%	>$19050 and ≤$77400	$ 1,905	>$9525 and ≤$38700	$ 952.50	>$13600 and ≤$51800	$ 1,360
22%	>$77400 and ≤$165000	$ 8,907	$38700 and ≤$82500	$ 4,453.50	>$51800 and ≤$82500	$ 5,944
24%	>$165000 and ≤$315000	$ 28,179	>$82500 and ≤$157500	$ 14,089.50	>$82500 and ≤$157500	$ 12,698
32%	>$315000 and ≤$400000	$ 64,179	>$157500 and ≤$200000	$ 32,089.50	>$157000 and ≤$200000	$ 30,698
35%	>$400,000 and <$600,000	$ 91,379	>$200000 and ≤$500000	$ 45,689.50	>$200000 and <$500000	$ 44,298
37%	>$600,000	$ 161,379	>$ 500,000	$ 150,689.50	>$500000	$ 140,298

Standard Deduction

The law also purports there is an enhanced standard deduction. This "enhanced" standard deduction is now set at $ 24K for joint filers and $ 12K for individual filers. (*If there is a qualifying child, meaning the taxpayer is the head of household, then the new standard deduction is $ 18K*).

Why would I use "purports"? Because the standard deduction has replaced the previous combination of a personal exemption and the old standard deduction. (The old standard deduction was $ 6350 for single taxpayers, $ 9250 for head of household filers, and $ 12700 for joint filers.)

This means for single taxpayers or heads of household with at least one qualifying child, the taxpayer is ahead. Compared to the old combination of standard deduction and personal exemption, there is a gain of some $ 2K of deductions. (But, if one were already itemizing, this new standard deduction raises the bar- because any itemized deductions must exceed $ 24,000 in value, considerably higher than $ 6350 for single persons or $ 9250 for heads of household.

The situation is different if one were married with two or more children. Because the old law, with the combined personal exemption and standard deduction was at least $ 28,000. Now, the new combined deduction is $ 24,000. And, if the taxpayer family had itemized deductions, they only had to exceed $ 12,700- now, they have to exceed $ 24,000 for the taxpayer to be able to itemize. (In particular, this may end up reducing the amount of charity folks donate, since it generally won't be deductible for those of moderate to middle-class means.)

Alternative Minimum Tax
(Yes, this is on a different form- but it does manipulate the tax rates)

The original concept behind the tax code change was to terminate the alternative minimum tax (AMT). But, after the initial bills were proposed, the AMT found its way back into the new law.

Unfortunately, the AMT has deviated dramatically from its original concept. It was supposed to be a means to collect more tax from wealthy individuals who received expert tax advice and employed various tax strategies. (Remember- one person's tax strategy is another person's tax loophole.) But, in execution, the AMT has been primarily applied against those taxpayers in the middle class.

The new law's provisions are not much different. The AMT exemptions (this means the levels below which they won't take effect) for individual taxpayers are $ 70,300, for married filing separately the exemption cut in at $ 54,700; and for married couples and surviving spouses, their incomes won't be subject to AMT once their adjusted gross income exceeds $ 109,400. The AMT phases out when married couples make more than $ 1,000,000 and $ 500,000 for everyone else. (In other words, the top 2% income earners never get hit with AMT.)

Which brings up some more real facts. Under the new law, by CY 2026, some 45% of those in the middle class (family income ranging between $ 50K and $ 160K) would be paying higher taxes than they did this year. But 1/3 would still be paying more than they did in 2018. Those taking the biggest financial hit? Families with children, to the tune of about $ 2K a year.

Educator Benefit

One of the good things about the compromise bill that became the law. The final version includes the $ 250 deduction teachers could use to compensate them (to some small degree' most teachers spend about 4X that amount) for all the funds teachers spend each year to provide the outstanding experience they want their students to receive. And, for which the school systems fail to provide. This is an above the line deduction. An above the line deduction means the $

250 is removed from the adjusted gross income is finalized, lowering the taxable income of the taxpayer.

Moreover, this benefit is now indexed for inflation.

Minimum Essential Health Coverage

The final version of the act repealed the provision that heretofore required taxpayers to maintain the minimum essential health coverage. (This is a concept developed under the Patient Protection and Affordable Care Act, PPACA; commonly referred to as Obamacare.) The problem was that the penalty was not high enough in the first place, and, by removing the requirement to be covered by health insurance, taxpayers are now able to game the system. Given that pre-existing conditions no longer preclude one from obtaining insurance, taxpayers now have the ability to wait until the last-minute (presumable after they are sick) to purchase insurance, much to the financial cost of the health insurers.

Should I Change My Withholdings?

By now, you may have been contacted by your employer to change your federal and state exemptions. Both because it's a new year- and because of the tax law that was enacted last year. Normally, you can follow the instructions that you are provided. (But NEVER choose 9 or more exemptions- even if you think that makes sense, because that sets off alarms with every tax agency. I'm not saying you are wrong- I am just saying, why bring on the aggravation.)

This year, the IRS is guessing how to advise taxpayers to choose exemptions. Both because they have been starved for qualified employees (the GOP is angry that the IRS collects fees from those folks who fail to sign up for the mandated [until next year] health insurance and for the incorrect assumption that the IRS chose to penalize social welfare (yeah, if you believe that, it's time for you buy all those bridges I don't own in Arizona, because I need some real social welfare) organizations that were really camouflaged political action groups for the GOP. (I'm not saying that the IRS didn't investigate these charades- just that they did the same investigation for the Democratic malarkey artists who claimed these organizations for their own goals.)

Oh, and there may be political reasons why the IRS may be providing inaccurate information. That way folks will think they are really getting bigger tax breaks than the law provides. (Don't get me wrong right here- they WILL generally have a lower tax bill- and in a few cases, as we will see, dramatically lower federal taxes.)

The problem is, if they choose the wrong bracket, they won't find out about those **errors** until after the election in November. As a matter of fact, they won't realize the potential problems until they file taxes sometime in March or April of next year- and find they owe money.

Why am I saying that? Because too many folks are forgetting that their state and property tax deductions are limited. So, they need to adjust their withholdings accordingly.   Let's consider five examples.

Our first example is a married couple. John and Mary are married and have two kids. Each parent grosses $ 60K. Their state taxes withheld are $ 7000, their property taxes are $ 6000, and their mortgage interest is $ 5000.

Frank is a single fellow who makes $ 150K in New York City. His state and local tax withholdings are $ 15K and he rents his abode.

Carol is a single mom, who makes $ 95K, and has two wonderful kids. Her mortgage interest is $ 7000, her property taxes are $ 6500 and her withheld state taxes are $ 8000.

And, finally, to see what happens when one's kids are in college, we'll add two more examples.

The first couple, Bob and Petunia are two older government workers. Their two kids are both in college. Each parent makes $ 125K, with state taxes of $ 9K, property taxes of $ 12K, $16K in mortgage interest, and $ 25K in tuition payments.

The last couple are Larry and Donna. All their expenses are the same as Bob and Petunia, except their gross income isn't $ 250K, but only $ 200K.

And, what do we find? The state tax burden has increased- sometimes dramatically. Why? Because the states have not adjusted their tax rules to meet the new Federal choices. And, since states assumed that many of their residents would itemize and would certainly have personal exemptions that no longer obtains (*given the eradication of individual exemptions at the federal level and the changed standard exemption*), the state tax burdens are higher.

2017	Gross Income	Standard Deduction	Mortgage Interest	SALT	Property Taxes	Exemptions	Federal Taxable	State Taxable	Tuition Credit	Child Credit	1040 Tax	State Income Tax	Total
John & Mary	120000	12700	5000	7000	6000	16200	85000	86500	0	2000	11102	4716	15818
Frank	150000	6350	0	15000	0	4050	130950	145950	0	0	29647	9206	18853
Carol	95000	9350	7000	8000	6500	12150	61150	69350	0	2000	9090	3270	12360
Bob & Petunia	250000	12700	16000	9000	22000	16200	196800	205800	0	0	41988	9261	51249
Larry & Donna	200000	12700	16000	9000	22000	16200	146800	155800	3000	0	23177	7011	20788

2018	Gross Income	Standard Deduction	Mortgage Interest	SALT	Property Taxes	Exemptions	Federal Taxable	State Taxable	Tuition Credit	Child Credit	1040 Tax	State Income Tax	Total
John & Mary	120000	24000	3000	7000	6000	0	96000	110800	0	4000	9219	5585	14804
Frank	150000	12000	0	15000	0	0	138000	145950	0	0	16663	12620	29283
Carol	95000	18000	7000	8000	6500	0	77000	89600	0	4000	364	4564	4968
Bob & Petunia	250000	24000	15000	9000	12000	0	226000	223800	0	4000	17987	12052	29969
Larry & Donna	200000	24000	16000	9000	12000	0	174000	194800	0	4000	6897	10765	17509

Notice how many folks can't itemize in 2018 (the standard deduction is in italics, when that is the case)

As you can see, Carol, the single mom, really saves a significant amount of money. But, every single example has a lower federal tax bill. But, no matter the scenario, the state tax burden increases.

Please note that I didn't include those folks with pass-through incomes. Or, significant capital gains. Because those situations (especially if the taxpayer were a lawyer or doctor) have significant "gotchas"!

So, be careful. Try out various scenarios to determine what your tax burden will be under the new tax rules. And, choose accordingly.

It's now how much we make-it's how we make it

Now you can see that this law means HOW we make our money is going to be a lot more critical than HOW MUCH money we make. It no longer means that everyone with the same adjusted gross income will be paying the same amount of tax. How one makes it-via a pass-through business, via dividends, or via wages (in increasing order of taxes required) will set the taxes due.

Chapter 8: Credits

Child Credit

Under the old law (CY 2017, which tax had to be filed no later than 17 April 2018), the child tax credit was available to those whose taxable income was below $ 75K (singles, but $ 115K for marrieds). Once the $ 75K adjusted gross income limit was exceeded, the credit was reduced by $ 50 for each $ 1K of additional income, which meant the credit is gone completely for those with taxable incomes of $ 95K ($135K for married).

The 2017 credit was $ 1000 [and could have actually been a refund if one's tax liability was low (to the tune of 15% of earned income in excess of $ 3000)]. That credit has been increased under the new law to $ 2000 for each qualified child. And, the phase out limit will be raised to $200 K (or $400K for marrieds).

There also is a new $ 500 tax credit for each dependent (who do not qualify for the child tax credit) that has added to the mix. This applies to children to old for the child tax credit or non-child dependents of the taxpayer.

Importantly, the tax credits are refundable up to $ 1400 (with phaseouts). This was the provision in the Senate version of the bill that prevailed. The provision provides that the taxpayer(s) can receive a tax credit for their children, even if no tax is owed.

So, from 2018 through 2026, a family of four would be entitled to $3800 in tax credits (maximum), as opposed to $ 2000 under the previous law. This could ease the problem developed by removing personal exemptions (roughly $4050 per person) and changing the standard deduction ($12000) to $ 24000, as mentioned above in Chapter 1 of this section. The $ 4200 of additional taxable income, assuming all the credits are earned, could be counterbalanced by the new tax credit.

A key fact to remember- no tax credit can be obtained if there is no social security number for the individual that is earning the credit for the filer.

Special Credits

For those over 65 who were entitled to credits ($5K for singles, $7.5K for marrieds) on their retirement or disability payments will no longer receive that 15% tax credit on those funds, under the new law.

Nor will there be an adoption credit ($ 13,750), or private activity bond credits. (While this wasn't a credit, the funds used by employers who helped pay for adoptions by their staff will now be taxable income to the employee.)

The higher education benefits (with a plethora of different names and provisions) shall be coalesced into one credit. The new version of the education credit will be 100% tax credit for the first $ 2K of qualified expenses and 25% for the next $ 2K.

Coverdell Savings Accounts that could cover some educational expenses would no longer be allowed. They actually would remain in force- but taxpayers can't add any money to them. And, taxpayers can roll those funds over into 529 or ABLE plans.

What PL 115-97 has really done is make 529's more like the terminated Coverdells, since 529 plans can now be used for elementary and high school educations (up to $10K of tuition is covered), as would be apprenticeship program tuitions. And, unborn children can be beneficiaries, now.

When student debt is forgiven by the lender, that amount had been charged as income to the taxpayer. Under PL 115-97, there will be a slight break to folks in that situation. Disabled taxpayers who get the debt forgiven or folks who die and have the debt forgiven will not have tax consequences. (*Yes- that really was the law of the land in 2017 and prior years!*)

The deduction for Interest on student debt payments, which is limited to $ 2500 a year, is still allowed- up to a point. (*The House version would not have allowed student loan interest to be deductible at all.*) The higher one's income, the less the deduction. Once one's income exceeds $ 65000 ($ 135K for married taxpayers), this benefit begins phasing out; it's gone completely when one's income exceeds $ 80K (or $ 165K for married couples).

The electric car credit has NOT been terminated. (*Admittedly, both Tesla and GM are reaching the maximum credit levels [200K cars sold] under the program. Which really means this credit extension will be a boon to Chinese-owned Volvo and German-owned Volkswagen, but not for American car manufacturers.*)

The last-minute change recognized an important fact. When the Georgia state credit expired, electric car sales dropped from 1400 a month to barely 100.

Extending this lost credit scenario to the whole US meant that car manufacturers will, at least for a short time, will not lose even more money per car (since some states mandate a set number of electric vehicles to be sold). Right now, it seems Tesla is losing a ton on each car (with investment included, the total loss per car is more than $ 50K) and GM is losing $ 9K per Volt sold. Not a good foreboding for zero emissions vehicles. [*By the way, coal won't work for car propulsion (unless it's converted to natural gas or some other fuel type).*]

Chapter 9. Schedule A Itemized Deductions

The biggest change for itemized deductions is the removal of limitation on itemized deductions for those making more money. Under the old tax laws, there was a throttling of allowable itemized deductions when one's adjusted gross income met or exceeded $261,500 (or $313,800 for marrieds). Under the new law, that limitation on deductibility totally disappears. *(But, there are changes to the various components of the deductions, as we'll see below.)*

As you can see from the table below, about 30% of taxpayers had itemized deductions under the old law. But, for those states that voted for Donald Trump, fewer taxpayers did so. For those states whose citizenry voted for Hilary Clinton, the number of taxpayers who itemized were generally a much higher percentage.

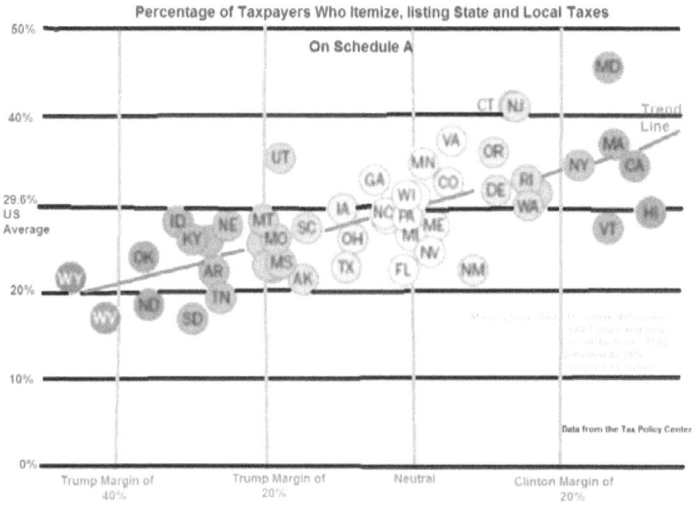

This chart will look dramatically different over the next five years.

But, with the higher standard deduction (and the loss of personal exemptions, plus the limitation on SALT that we will discuss below), this picture will be dramatically different. Before, one could deduct mortgage interest, state and local taxes (SALT), charitable deductions (and a few other items) when those totals exceeded the standard deduction. For single folks, that meant itemizing made sense if one had deductions that exceeded $6350. Married folks filing jointly only had to exceed $ 12700 of deductions to benefit. Given mortgage interest of $ 5000, state income taxes of $ 1000 to $ 2000, property taxes of $ 5000 (all these numbers are on the very low end), it was easy to do. So, folks would also donate money to charity, since – besides the benefit to our society- the after-tax costs would be significantly below the outlay.

Now, a married couple will have to have those costs exceed $ 24K to be deductible. And, when one realizes that state and local income taxes, plus property taxes are limited to a deductibility of $ 10K, those folks itemizing deductions will be greatly reduced from the previous 30% of all taxpayers.

Mortgage Interest and Total Mortgage Indebtedness

The previous tax law afforded one the ability to deduct mortgage interest as long as the total indebtedness was under $ 1 KKK. (Home equity debt or lines of credit were additionally limited; a total amount of $ 100,000 was allowed.) Those amounts will continue to be allowed*, but any mortgage interest on NEW debt (assuming there is no other mortgage debt) will be subjected to a $ 750K (total) mortgage indebtedness limit. *(Guess what? Only one home mortgage interest will be deductible, now. No NEW second homes or vacation homes. Which is why there was an asterisk (allowed*) describing the current situation that may be maintainable.)*

There is another mortgage provision that was changed by the new law. Up until this year, mortgage insurance premiums were deductible as if they were mortgage interest payments. The new law removed the deductibility of these payment.

(Not quite a provision, but should a taxpayer fallen on hard times, and the bank foreclosed on his/her property, it was possible to have the mortgage debt that the bank didn't collect be forgiven. That no longer applies. If one receives a 1099-C for mortgage debt, the taxpayer will have to include that amount of debt forbearance within the taxable income as filed on Form 1040.)

Refinancing and HELOC (Home Equity Line of Credit)

Here's the kicker. You know that refinance you just finessed? Oh, there's a problem with that. Or, maybe not. Because that refinancing- the one that brought you a check as you increased your debt? You better be able to prove that you used that money to improve your home, putting on an extension, etc. Because if you used it to buy a car, pay down credit card debt, or similar pursuits- the IRS considers that to be generally non-deductible. So, only part of your mortgage interest is going to be deductible on Schedule A (Itemized Deductions).

Two examples may make this rule clearer.

Example 1: You bought your home some years ago for $ 750K and put down $ 150 K to purchase it. So, your $ 600K mortgage has been paid down to $ 293K. And, now you just borrowed $ 440K. This covered the student loan debt for your kids, your credit card debt, leaving you with a fresh start.

Um. Not quite. You see your "acquisition debt" is still $ 293K (the balance of the original mortgage). And, you can only use up to $ 100K for home equity. So, that debt you took on over $ 393K is not deductible. Only 89.3% of your mortgage interest is deductible.

Example 2: Same house, same payment. But, you only borrowed $ 366K, using the excess to pay for a new car ($44,300), pay down credit card debt ($25K), and pay points on the new mortgage ($3.7K). As you can determine, your "acquisition debt" is the same ($293K), but the total extra amount borrowed is less than $100K. Since your additional home equity debt does not exceed $ 100K, your entire mortgage is still deductible.

Maybe it's time you read Publication 936. Because it's your money at risk.

State Income Taxes, Real Estate Taxes, and Property Taxes

Oh, and property taxes? They'll only be deductible up to $ 10K a year. And, no property taxes on foreign property will be deductible, either. Sorry Californians and New Yorkers (among other high property tax locales). Moreover, while only 2.5% of Americans have (or may need) mortgages in excess of $500K, the bulk of those folks live in California, New Jersey, and New York- and the cities of Boston (MA) and Washington (DC). You know- the places that don't generally vote for the GOP.

(As a result of this targeted hit, many states are considering suing the federal government over these changes. (I don't think they will have much success, by the way.) But, at least as many are getting creative. They are planning to incorporate an employer payroll tax that will replace the state income taxes. (A payroll tax would be deductible under the law. State income taxes are not deductible.) Others are considering allowing payments to the state government to be charitable deductions. [That means there would be no SALT limitation; those payments would be allowed as charitable deductions!])

What May Happen With SALT Deductions

We have heard from several politicians that claim it's the Blue States that are hurting the economy- neglecting to mention that it's the Red States who take more money from the Feds (to balance their budgets) than they put in. Most of the Blue States provide the federal treasury significantly higher levels of funding than they may receive in benefits. But, that won't stop those states whose citizens are going to lose significant deductions to find new ways around the rules.

This is why New York and New Jersey (among other states) are considering new provisions to "bypass' the SALT limitation. (*We are talking about that $10,000 maximum SALT – state and local taxes- deduction limit.*)

While it's not clear how many employers are enthused with the New York state response, I'm betting they'll be on board in droves- assuming it survives a Federal challenge. Because the companies will save money, too. (*There will need to be some adjustment to union contracts- and determining what happens when folks live in different states than where they are employed.*) The deadline for them to sign on is 1 December 2018 for CY 2019.

Without this adjustment, a bit more than 8% of the folks who live in New York will get zapped by an average of $3340 (due to the SALT limitations). So, New York invented a new state payroll tax. Should the employer join the deal, the amounts deducted will count towards the employee's state income tax. And, employers get to deduct these amounts against their federal income taxes. (*Businesses have no limitation on SALT payments.*)

Oh, yeah. Employers will be lowering folks' pay checks, but their net pay [take-home] will still be the same. (*In other words, less pre-tax income, but with the lower federal tax bite, there will be the same or more after-tax income.*)

Basically, the system in New York works as follows. For those folks whose wages exceed $ 40,000, there is a new (optional) payroll tax of 1.5% (*which will rise to 5% by 2021; the phase-in period is to allow folks to have a chance to adjust to the change in net and gross payroll*). Once the 5% max is operational, someone whose wages were $ 100,000 would have the ability to save $ 700 by this scheme, even though his new payroll would be $ 97,000.

The problem for multi-state corporations is explaining why someone who is working in Florida will have a payroll level of $ 100K, while this NY employee earns $ 3K less. Also, pre-tax wages set up Social Security benefits (*trust me, a $ 3K drop in payroll at $ 100K won't affect one's monthly checks on retirement by much*), but it does affect 401(k) matching contributions and limitations. Plus, the employee's self-regard with that lower salary.

And, then, there's the New Jersey response. Their concept is to let taxpayers proffer charitable donations to cities, counties, local government entities, and school boards in lieu of paying taxes. Since there is no limit on charitable donations (ok, there is, but none of these folks will be shelling out 50% of their income to pay these "charitable deductions"), the SALT payment limitations won't be a problem.

As opposed to the New York solution, the Jersey concept has a problem- at least to me. After all, when we donate $100 to NPR and they provide us with an ugly coffee cup that they claim is worth $10, we only get to deduct $90 as charitable contributions. Isn't donating $2K to the school board and getting a $2K benefit ensuring that we have no valid charitable deduction?

Now, Drs. Joseph Bankman and Jacob Goldin (both from Stanford), David Gamage (Indian University), Daniel Jacob Hemel (U Chicago), Darien Shanske and Dennis J. Ventry (UC Davis), Kirk J. Stark (UCLA), and Manoj Viswanathan (UC Hastings) feel this approach is valid, and have developed a 44 page monograph explaining their thinking. (*Just so you know, this isn't really about New Jersey, but covers the 113 such programs that already exist in 32 states and DC where this practice has already been condoned. After all, if Alabamians and West Virginians can donate to scholarship funds and don't have to reduce the value of their donations by the value received, so can Jerseyites.*)

> Guidance on Certain Payments Made in Exchange for State and Local Tax Credits
>
> NOTICE 2018-54
>
> SECTION 1. PURPOSE
>
> This notice informs taxpayers that the Department of the Treasury (Treasury Department) and the Internal Revenue Service (IRS) intend to propose regulations addressing the federal income tax treatment of certain payments made by taxpayers for which taxpayers receive a credit against their state and local taxes
>
> SECTION 2. BACKGROUND
>
> Section 11042 of "The Tax Cuts and Jobs Act," Pub. L. No. 115-97, limits an individual's deduction under § 164 for the aggregate amount of state and local taxes paid during the calendar year to $10,000 ($5,000 in the case of a married individual filing a separate return). State and local tax payments in excess of those amounts are not deductible. This new limitation applies to taxable years beginning after December 31, 2017, and before January 1, 2026.
>
> In response to this new limitation, some state legislatures are considering or have adopted legislative proposals that would allow taxpayers to make transfers to funds controlled by state or local governments, or other transferees specified by the state, in exchange for credits against the state or local taxes that the taxpayer is required to pay. The aim of these proposals is to allow taxpayers to characterize such

And, of course, the IRS takes issue with this. (*Yes, even though- at least in New Jersey's case- the solution chosen is one the IRS has allowed for years.*)

Court Judgments

This is one of those hidden gems. One I missed when I read the Tax Cuts and Jobs Act. (Now you know why my monograph on the law hasn't been published yet. I'm still re-reading the verbiage to see if there are other "gems" (*a.k.a. fecal deposits*) hidden between the lines.)

Now, I have a way around this- I think. But, for now, I'm just sharing with y'all the sad news.

Let's assume I have a client who didn't pay his bill. (Let's hope this is a terrible assumption, OK.) And, my firm sues the creep. And, we collect the bill, interest, and legal fees. Under the new law, nothing has changed. If the lawyer collects the whole amount, s/he turns over our now-collected fees and the interest; the lawyer keeps the legal fees. If the lawyer also gets a percentage of the collection, then the lawyer keeps the portion to which we all agreed (hopefully), and we get the rest. We each pay taxes on the revenue we recognized.

(No, you can't quite claim you don't recall getting that $ 122,000 collection. Recognition here simply means the funds that were deposited into your bank account.)

If the lawsuit involved physical injury, then the lawyer pays taxes on the fees it receives for its efforts. And, the injured party gets to keep its portion of the recovery tax-free. Again, no change.

What about if you are suing your employer? Each of you (the law firm and you) pays taxes on the funds received. Unless, of course, the case involves sexual harassment or abuse. Well, not in all those cases- only when there is a non-disclosure clause or agreement. (*Oh, by the way. Have you ever seen one of those decisions that DOESN'T have a non-disclosure clause? Yeah. Neither have I.*) This new law also affects what happens if you bring suit for invasion of privacy? defamation? or, claims related to divorce or child support?

Here's the big surprise. In all these cases, we (the plaintiffs) get taxed on 100% of the decision. And, there is NO deduction for legal fees. Yes, this does mean that the IRS will be collecting taxes on some money TWICE. The lawyer still is responsible to pay taxes on the money it receives- and we pay taxes on the money we collect and money we don't (*the money that ends up in our lawyer's (or lawyers') pockets*).

It's not just those items. Trespass, bad investment or tax advice (stockbrokers or tax advisers), bad faith insurance company torts, wrongful arrest or imprisonment, emotional distress, legal malpractice, or punitive damages from a trucking firm or driver (*yep, that's there, too!*) are all on this new list of double taxation.

This change is a result of the annihilation of the miscellaneous itemized deduction (and deduction for itemized expenses) that was at the bottom of Schedule A, the itemized deduction form of the 1040. (*You can see where that appeared in the 2017 tax form, above.*)

543 U.S. 426

COMMISSIONER OF INTERNAL REVENUE
v.
BANKS

No. 03-892.

Supreme Court of United States.

Argued November 1, 2004
Decided January 24, 2005.

Respondent Banks settled his federal employment discrimination suit against a California state agency and respondent Banaitis settled his Oregon state case against his former employer, but neither included fees paid to their attorneys under contingent-fee agreements as gross income on their federal income tax returns. In each case petitioner Commissioner of Internal Revenue issued a notice of deficiency, which the Tax Court upheld. In Banks' case, the Sixth Circuit reversed in part, finding that the amount Banks paid to his attorney was not includable as gross income. In Banaitis' case, the Ninth Circuit found that because Oregon law grants attorneys a superior lien in the contingent-fee portion of any recovery, that part of Banaitis' settlement was not includable as gross income.

Held: When a litigant's recovery constitutes income, the litigant's income includes the portion of the recovery paid to the attorney as a contingent fee. Pp. 432-439.

(a) Two preliminary observations help clarify why this issue is of consequence. First, taking the legal expenses as miscellaneous itemized deductions would have been of no help to respondents because the Alternative Minimum Tax establishes a tax liability floor and does not allow such deductions. Second, the American Jobs Creation Act of 2004

Oh, and a 2005 court decision, Commissioner v. Banks. (*The commissioner in question is the IRS Commissioner, hence the tax effect- and don't consider it's not the law of the land, as would be true if it were a Tax Court result. This one is a US Supreme Court decision.*) SCOTUS decided that plaintiffs are required to recognize (*here's that term again*) 100% of the recovery as part of their gross income. (*Congress sought fit to modify this requirement by passing an above the line deduction for employment and (some) whistleblower claims.*)

It gets better (*or worse, depending on your point of view*). So many folks thought that if there are two checks issued- one to the lawyers and one to the plaintiff(s), that would solve the problem. Nope! That Banks decision, 543 U.S. 426 (2005) stipulates that the defendant is to issue a 1099 for the full settlement to the plaintiff.

So, before you agree to a contingent fee case, you better figure out how you are going to afford to pay the tax on any potential award.

Or, hope my wrinkle works out

Other Itemized Items

Deductions for charity would no longer be limited to 50% of one's adjusted gross income- that limit has been raised to 60%. Except, this means you need more than $ 24K of itemized deductions (between SALT, mortgage interest, medical, and charity) to begin itemizing. And, the gimmick about buying college athletic tickets and deducting the cost as a charitable donation- poof! It's gone.

Nor will we be able to deduct the cost of tax preparation. That's really not a big loss, since it had already been limited by the fact that there was a 2% threshold. (*Only the costs that exceed 2% of one's income were deductible.*) The same rule - non-deductibility- will also apply for expenses one incurs (and that are not reimbursed) due to one's employment. (In particular, this was where most union members deducted their dues.) These were also deductible above the 2% threshold. (*Actually, the tax prep AND non-reimbursed employee expenses were added together to determine that 2% threshold.*)

As stated above, medical expenses that do not exceed 7.5% of our adjusted gross income (with the threshold rising to 10% in CY 2019 and subsequent years) would also no longer be deductible. Oh, another thing. The payments made to Medical Savings Accounts would no longer be deductible. And, employer contributions to such accounts (MSA) would now be considered taxable income. (*It was deductible for the employer, but not taxable to the recipient; the MSA's let employers provide high deductible health insurance and use the MSA to cover the out-of-pocket expenses for their employees.*) Only Health Savings Accounts are now allowed. (Existing balances on an MSA are allowed to be rolled over into an HSA.)

The medical expense deduction was added back in because our elected officials were finally convinced how badly this would penalize seniors in a big way. Considering that almost 1/2 of those deducting medical expenses have family incomes under $ 50K (69% earn $ 75K or less), this was finally recognized as too big a hit to the lower middle class and senior citizens of the US.

Chapter 10: Other Personal Tax Provisions

Capital Gains

As has been true before, the tax on capital gains is dependent upon one's taxable income. The limits have been changed.

If one were filing jointly, there is no capital gains taxes for those amounts up to $ 77,200. Over that threshold, the tax rate is 15% until the gain reaches $ 479,000. Once the $ 479,000 level is exceeded, the capital gains tax rate becomes 20%.

Moreover, the net investment income tax, for those individuals whose gross adjusted income exceeds $ 200K (joint filers have a $ 250K threshold), is still in force. The rate remained at 3.8% on the lesser of net investment income or the amount the adjusted gross income exceeds the threshold..

Alimony, Moving, Theft and Casualty Losses

This specific provision is going to make divorce settlements a lot harder to achieve. But, at least, they extended the deadline that obtained in their proposed bills. Originally, anyone getting divorced after CY 2017 would no longer be able to deduct the cost of alimony from one's income nor could those funds be taxable income to the recipient. But, that provision has been extended a year. So, if you get divorced in

2019 or later, alimony won't be deductible for the payer or taxable to the recipient.

And, moving expenses will no longer reduce one's income. These costs will no longer be deductible. Worse yet- if the employer pays for the move to a new location (where they want you to be working), those payments are considered to be taxable income to the employee!

Theft and personal casualty losses- unless one lives in a certified disaster zone- would no longer be deductible from one's income, either.

Homes and Housing

Excluding the costs for employer provided housing would now be limited to $ 50K a year- but only if your earned income is $120K or less. The benefit will be phased out at the rate of 50 cents on the dollar for each dollar of earned income that exceeds $ 120K. Assuming one's income were $220K or more, the deduction would be totally disallowed and taxable to the recipient.

Selling our homes will become more expensive, too. Right now, we can exclude $ 500K (married; half that for singles) of the gains on the sale of our homes from our taxable income- as long as this house was our primary residence for 2 of the past 5 years. The rule would become 5 of the past 8 years- and the capital gains exclusion would be limited in use to once every 5 years! Oh, it gets worse. That capital gains exclusion would be limited by $1 for every dollar of taxable income above $ 500K. (Singles currently get $ 250K- and the benefit will be erased as their income exceeds $ 250K, dollar for dollar.)

Chapter 11. The New 1040

To further convince you how great this tax change is, the Feds have been revising the tax forms we must submit. (*I admit that most of us use electronic filing [89%!!!], so we really don't pay attention to the forms, but this is for advertising and "attaboys" for the new tax plan.*)

In so doing, the IRS has cut the size of the 1040 form dramatically. But, really, that smaller form just means you must fill out a bunch of other schedules and forms, which had never exited or been required before.

So, let's compare the forms.

As you can see from the 2017 1040 form on the next two pages, there are 79 items that may or may not be filled in. But, the whole bottom of page 1 has disappeared when we see the new 1040. (*Hold on- that's not really true- but we'll get to that.*)

Form 1040 — U.S. Individual Income Tax Return (2017)

Department of the Treasury—Internal Revenue Service (99)
OMB No. 1545-0074 IRS Use Only—Do not write or staple in this space.

For the year Jan. 1–Dec. 31, 2017, or other tax year beginning _____, 2017, ending _____, 20____ See separate instructions.

Your first name and initial | Last name | Your social security number

If a joint return, spouse's first name and initial | Last name | Spouse's social security number

Home address (number and street). If you have a P.O. box, see instructions. | Apt. no. | ▲ Make sure the SSN(s) above and on line 6c are correct.

City, town or post office, state, and ZIP code. If you have a foreign address, also complete spaces below (see instructions).

Presidential Election Campaign
Check here if you, or your spouse if filing jointly, want $3 to go to this fund. Checking a box below will not change your tax or refund. ☐ You ☐ Spouse

Foreign country name | Foreign province/state/county | Foreign postal code

Filing Status
Check only one box.
1. ☐ Single
2. ☐ Married filing jointly (even if only one had income)
3. ☐ Married filing separately. Enter spouse's SSN above and full name here. ▶
4. ☐ Head of household (with qualifying person). (See instructions.) If the qualifying person is a child but not your dependent, enter this child's name here. ▶
5. ☐ Qualifying widow(er) (see instructions)

Exemptions
6a ☐ **Yourself.** If someone can claim you as a dependent, **do not** check box 6a . . . . . .
b ☐ **Spouse** . . . .

c Dependents:
(1) First name Last name | (2) Dependent's social security number | (3) Dependent's relationship to you | (4) ✓ if child under age 17 qualifying for child tax credit (see instructions)

If more than four dependents, see instructions and check here ▶ ☐

Boxes checked on 6a and 6b ____
No. of children on 6c who:
• lived with you ____
• did not live with you due to divorce or separation (see instructions) ____
Dependents on 6c not entered above ____
Add numbers on lines above ▶ ____

d Total number of exemptions claimed . . . .

Income

Attach Form(s) W-2 here. Also attach Forms W-2G and 1099-R if tax was withheld.

If you did not get a W-2, see instructions.

7 Wages, salaries, tips, etc. Attach Form(s) W-2 . . . . | 7
8a Taxable interest. Attach Schedule B if required . . . . | 8a
b Tax-exempt interest. **Do not** include on line 8a . . . | 8b |
9a Ordinary dividends. Attach Schedule B if required . . . . | 9a
b Qualified dividends . . . . | 9b |
10 Taxable refunds, credits, or offsets of state and local income taxes . . . . . . | 10
11 Alimony received . . . . | 11
12 Business income or (loss). Attach Schedule C or C-EZ . . . . | 12
13 Capital gain or (loss). Attach Schedule D if required. If not required, check here ▶ ☐ | 13
14 Other gains or (losses). Attach Form 4797 . . . . | 14
15a IRA distributions . | 15a | b Taxable amount . . . | 15b
16a Pensions and annuities | 16a | b Taxable amount . . . | 16b
17 Rental real estate, royalties, partnerships, S corporations, trusts, etc. Attach Schedule E | 17
18 Farm income or (loss). Attach Schedule F . . . . | 18
19 Unemployment compensation . . . . | 19
20a Social security benefits | 20a | b Taxable amount . . . | 20b
21 Other income. List type and amount _____ | 21
22 Combine the amounts in the far right column for lines 7 through 21. This is your **total income** ▶ | 22

Adjusted Gross Income

23 Educator expenses . . . . | 23
24 Certain business expenses of reservists, performing artists, and fee-basis government officials. Attach Form 2106 or 2106-EZ | 24
25 Health savings account deduction. Attach Form 8889 . | 25
26 Moving expenses. Attach Form 3903 . . . . . . | 26
27 Deductible part of self-employment tax. Attach Schedule SE . | 27
28 Self-employed SEP, SIMPLE, and qualified plans . . | 28
29 Self-employed health insurance deduction . . . . | 29
30 Penalty on early withdrawal of savings . . . . . | 30
31a Alimony paid b Recipient's SSN ▶ _____ | 31a
32 IRA deduction . . . . | 32
33 Student loan interest deduction . . . . | 33
34 Tuition and fees. Attach Form 8917 . . . . | 34
35 Domestic production activities deduction. Attach Form 8903 | 35
36 Add lines 23 through 35 . . . . | 36
37 Subtract line 36 from line 22. This is your **adjusted gross income** . . . . . ▶ | 37

For Disclosure, Privacy Act, and Paperwork Reduction Act Notice, see separate instructions. Cat. No. 11320B Form **1040** (2017)

Form 1040 (2017) Page 2

Tax and Credits	38	Amount from line 37 (adjusted gross income)		38
	39a	Check if: ☐ You were born before January 2, 1953, ☐ Blind. ☐ Spouse was born before January 2, 1953, ☐ Blind. } Total boxes checked ▶ 39a		
	b	If your spouse itemizes on a separate return or you were a dual-status alien, check here ▶ 39b ☐		
Standard Deduction for—	40	Itemized deductions (from Schedule A) or your standard deduction (see left margin)		40
• People who check any box on line 39a or 39b or who can be claimed as a dependent, see instructions.	41	Subtract line 40 from line 38		41
	42	Exemptions. If line 38 is $156,900 or less, multiply $4,050 by the number on line 6d. Otherwise, see instructions		42
	43	Taxable income. Subtract line 42 from line 41. If line 42 is more than line 41, enter -0-		43
	44	Tax (see instructions). Check if any from: a ☐ Form(s) 8814 b ☐ Form 4972 c ☐		44
	45	Alternative minimum tax (see instructions). Attach Form 6251		45
• All others	46	Excess advance premium tax credit repayment. Attach Form 8962		46
Single or Married filing separately, $6,350	47	Add lines 44, 45, and 46 ▶		47
	48	Foreign tax credit. Attach Form 1116 if required	48	
Married filing jointly or Qualifying widow(er), $12,700	49	Credit for child and dependent care expenses. Attach Form 2441	49	
	50	Education credits from Form 8863, line 19	50	
	51	Retirement savings contributions credit. Attach Form 8880	51	
Head of household, $9,350	52	Child tax credit. Attach Schedule 8812, if required	52	
	53	Residential energy credits. Attach Form 5695	53	
	54	Other credits from Form: a ☐ 3800 b ☐ 8801 c ☐	54	
	55	Add lines 48 through 54. These are your total credits		55
	56	Subtract line 55 from line 47. If line 55 is more than line 47, enter -0- ▶		56
Other Taxes	57	Self-employment tax. Attach Schedule SE		57
	58	Unreported social security and Medicare tax from Form: a ☐ 4137 b ☐ 8919		58
	59	Additional tax on IRAs, other qualified retirement plans, etc. Attach Form 5329 if required		59
	60a	Household employment taxes from Schedule H		60a
	b	First-time homebuyer credit repayment. Attach Form 5405 if required		60b
	61	Health care: individual responsibility (see instructions) Full-year coverage ☐		61
	62	Taxes from: a ☐ Form 8959 b ☐ Form 8960 c ☐ Instructions; enter code(s)		62
	63	Add lines 56 through 62. This is your total tax ▶		63
Payments	64	Federal income tax withheld from Forms W-2 and 1099	64	
	65	2017 estimated tax payments and amount applied from 2016 return	65	
If you have a qualifying child, attach Schedule EIC.	66a	Earned income credit (EIC)	66a	
	b	Nontaxable combat pay election	66b	
	67	Additional child tax credit. Attach Schedule 8812	67	
	68	American opportunity credit from Form 8863, line 8	68	
	69	Net premium tax credit. Attach Form 8962	69	
	70	Amount paid with request for extension to file	70	
	71	Excess social security and tier 1 RRTA tax withheld	71	
	72	Credit for federal tax on fuels. Attach Form 4136	72	
	73	Credits from Form: a ☐ 2439 b ☐ Reserved c ☐ 8885 d ☐	73	
	74	Add lines 64, 65, 66a, and 67 through 73. These are your total payments ▶		74
Refund	75	If line 74 is more than line 63, subtract line 63 from line 74. This is the amount you overpaid		75
	76a	Amount of line 75 you want refunded to you. If Form 8888 is attached, check here ▶ ☐		76a
Direct deposit? See instructions.	▶ b	Routing number	▶ c Type: ☐ Checking ☐ Savings	
	▶ d	Account number		
	77	Amount of line 75 you want applied to your 2018 estimated tax ▶	77	
Amount You Owe	78	Amount you owe. Subtract line 74 from line 63. For details on how to pay, see instructions ▶		78
	79	Estimated tax penalty (see instructions)	79	
Third Party Designee	Do you want to allow another person to discuss this return with the IRS (see instructions)? ☐ Yes. Complete below. ☐ No Designee's name ▶ Phone no. ▶ Personal identification number (PIN) ▶			
Sign Here Joint return? See instructions. Keep a copy for your records.	Under penalties of perjury, I declare that I have examined this return and accompanying schedules and statements, and to the best of my knowledge and belief, they are true, correct, and accurately list all amounts and sources of income I received during the tax year. Declaration of preparer (other than taxpayer) is based on all information of which preparer has any knowledge. Your signature Date Your occupation Daytime phone number Spouse's signature. If a joint return, both must sign. Date Spouse's occupation If the IRS sent you an Identity Protection PIN, enter it here (see inst.)			
Paid Preparer Use Only	Print/Type preparer's name Preparer's signature Date Check ☐ if self-employed PTIN Firm's name ▶ Firm's EIN ▶ Firm's address ▶ Phone no.			

[Form 1040 Simplified, U.S. Individual Income Tax Return, 2018 — image of the form]

But, page 1 of the new 1040, as shown above? Oops. There's nothing to compute on this page. We just have to fill in our names and our dependents (*of course, we need to add the social security numbers for everyone*), and our signatures (*as well as the identity and signature of the preparers we use.*)

Oh, yeah, to make the form look simpler, these requests are not numbered. So, POOF! We've lowered the number of lines by 6- doing absolutely nothing to make the taxes simpler or easier.

[Form 1040 (2018), Page 2 shown]

Page 2 of the new 1040 (*shown directly above*) now requires the information that was present on the old form in lines 7 through 9- our salaries, our dividends, our interest, and on lines 15 and 16 that detailed our pensions, IRAs, and social security. So, the 1040 is shorter- there's a total of 23 items (*plus the 6 that aren't counted, remember?*), instead of 79.

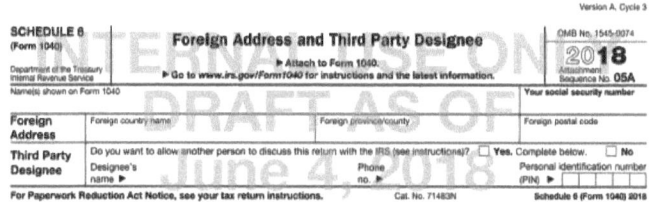

Now, how has this legerdemain been accomplished? Oh, by requiring taxpayers to complete up to SIX new, separate schedules. Admittedly, most folks won't need Schedule 6 (*which covers a third-party designee and foreign addresses*).

SCHEDULE 5 (Form 1040) — Other Payments and Refundable Credits

OMB No. 1545-0074
2018
Attachment Sequence No. 05

Department of the Treasury — Internal Revenue Service

▶ Attach to Form 1040.
▶ Go to www.irs.gov/Form1040 for instructions and the latest information.

Name(s) shown on Form 1040 | Your social security number

Other Payments and Refundable Credits

Line	Description	Amount
65	Reserved	65
66	2018 estimated tax payments and amount applied from 2017 return	66
67a	Reserved	67a
b	Reserved	67b
68–69	Reserved	68–69
70	Net premium tax credit. Attach Form 8962	70
71	Amount paid with request for extension to file (see instructions)	71
72	Excess social security and tier 1 tax withheld	72
73	Credit for federal tax on fuels. Attach Form 4136	73
74a	Amounts from Form 2439	74a
b	Health coverage tax credit. Attach Form 8885	74b
c	Reserved	74c
d	Other amounts (see instructions)	74d
75	Add lines 65, 66, 67a, and 68 through 74. These are your total **other payments and refundable credits**. Enter here and on Form 1040, line 17d	75

For Paperwork Reduction Act Notice, see your tax return instructions. Cat. No. 71482C Schedule 5 (Form 1040) 2018

INTERNAL USE ONLY — DRAFT AS OF June 5, 2018

Schedule 5 (above) will only be needed by those who get a health insurance tax credit (*and underpaid or overpaid according to the credit given and deserved*), excess social security taxes withheld (*those with two or more jobs*), and to reconcile payments filed with extensions to file. Schedule 2 *(below) will* be needed by those subject to AMT (*alternative minimum tax- which requires a whole bunch of computations*), and those health care credit payments- so not many of us will need to deal with this, either.

Schedule 1 (*below*) includes all those things on the bottom of the old 1040, page 1. Plus, a few from the top of page 1- those of us who are self-employed, have rental properties, pass-through entities, and farms will have to compute the data behind these questions. That is a whole bunch of us.

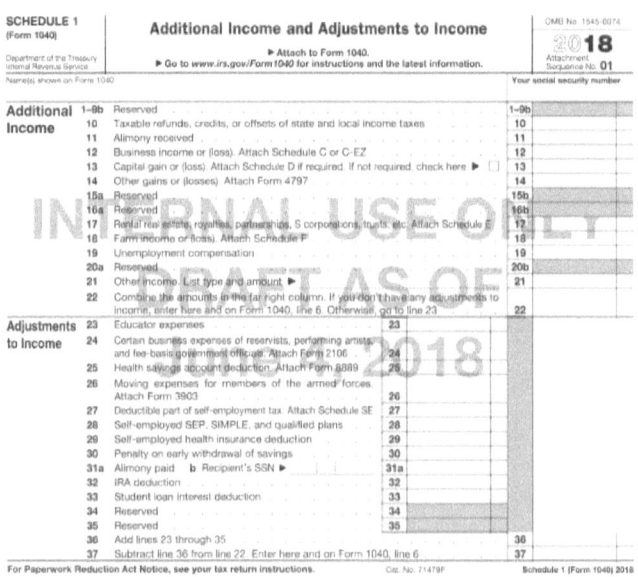

Schedule 3 (below) will also be used by a bunch of folks- it covers child tax credits and child care expenses. As well as education credits and contributions to be deducted for our retirement plans, among other such items.

SCHEDULE 3 (Form 1040)
Department of the Treasury
Internal Revenue Service

Nonrefundable Credits

▶ Attach to Form 1040.
▶ Go to www.irs.gov/Form1040 for instructions and the latest information.

OMB No. 1545-0074

2018

Attachment Sequence No. 03

Name(s) shown on Form 1040

Your social security number

Nonrefundable Credits			
48	Foreign tax credit. Attach Form 1116 if required	48	
49	Credit for child and dependent care expenses. Attach Form 2441	49	
50	Education credits from Form 8863, line 19	50	
51	Retirement savings contributions credit. Attach Form 8880	51	
52	Child tax credit and credit for other dependents	52	
53	Residential energy credit. Attach Form 5695	53	
54a	General business credit. Attach Form 3800	54a	
b	Credit for prior year minimum tax. Attach Form 8801	54b	
c	Other credits (see instructions)	54c	
55	Add lines 48 through 54. These are your **total nonrefundable credits.** Enter here and on Form 1040, line 12	55	

For Paperwork Reduction Act Notice, see your tax return instructions. Cat. No. 71480G Schedule 3 (Form 1040) 2018

INTERNAL USE ONLY
DRAFT AS OF
June 5, 2018

Schedule 4 (*below*) will be used by the self-employed and the wealthy (*to determine those dreaded extra Medicare and Social Security taxes*). Plus, for those of us who have household employees, this schedule addresses the taxes due for that situation.

So, in reality, the tax forms are not really simpler. We (*that's the government*) just want to fool you into thinking they are.

And, you can rest assured that the IRS is betting a whole bunch of us will miss the deductions and other items that were found on the old page 1. And, that includes the Earned Income Credit (*EIC*), which is abbreviated- and many of those so entitled don't really use the abbreviation. Another big OOPS.

Internal Revenue Service
DEPARTMENT OF THE TREASURY

1040EZ2DO - Tax Form
New Simplified Tax Form

1. How Much Money Did You Make? $_____

2. Send It to Us.

At least- this is what many politicians want you to believe!

Postscript

If you would like to research further any aspect of the new law, the text can be found here.

www.ingramcontent.com/pod-product-compliance
Lightning Source LLC
Chambersburg PA
CBHW031437210526
45464CB00005B/2237